UFO

Secrets Revealed

Phil Cousineau

HarperCollins*West*
A Division of HarperCollins*Publishers*

Front Cover Design: Bob Albert
Photograph: © Fujio Nakahashi/Tony Stone Images
Interior Design: Bob Albert & Annie Kook

ISBN: 0-06-258652-1

95 96 97 98 99 ❖ RDD(H) 10 9 8 7 6 5 4 3 2 1

⊗ A TREE CLAUSE BOOK

HarperCollins West and the author, in association with The Basic Foundation, a not-for-profit organization whose primary mission is reforestation, will facilitate the planting of two trees for every one tree used in the manufacture of this book.

This edition is printed on acid-free paper that meets the American National Standards Institute Z39.48 Standard.

To Jo
with uforia

A UFO is the reported sighting of an object or light seen in the sky or on land, whose appearance, trajectory, actions, motions, lights, and colors do not have a logical, conventional, or natural explanation, and which cannot be explained, not only by the original witness, but by scientists or technical experts who try to make a common sense identification after examining the evidence.
    —J. Allen Hynek, the Center for UFO Studies (CUFOS)

In that sublime moment I knew the mystery of life.
                    —UFO contactee Orfeo Antalucci, describing
                        his encounter with a flying saucer

So now these UFOs are appearing in the skies. Although they have always been observed they didn't signify anything. Now suddenly they seem to portend something—a hope, an expectation.
                    —Carl Gustav Jung, *Flying Saucers*

Contents

Acknowledgments

I would like to express my gratitude to my friends at HarperCollins West who helped me navigate this book home, especially my editor, Shirley Christine, for being a wise guide and shrewd interpreter of the mysteries; Beth Weber, for keeping the project on the radar screen; and Annie Kook and Bob Albert, for their levitating book design. My deep gratitude also to Linda Berlin, for her diligent research; Karin Mullen, for her vigilant copyediting; and Brenda Knight, for believing that this ship could fly.

For their valuable assistance, I would also like to acknowledge John Timmerman of the Center for UFO Studies, who graciously supplied us with several key questions, sources, and photographs; Mark Weiman of Regent Press for permission to reprint several images from his book; Tom Morgan of the Mary Evans Picture Library; Glenn Campbell, the indefatigable researcher and watchdog in Nevada, for his insights into Area 51; Jerry McCormack of the *Roswell Daily Record*, for granting permission to reprint the headline for the article on the Corona Crash; David C. Burgevin of the Smithsonian Institution for his photo research; Abe Dane from *Popular Mechanics*, for his help in procuring military photographs; Professor David Jacobs for providing valuable background material; and John Price of the Outa Limits UFO Enigma Museum in Roswell, New Mexico, for his gracious hospitality and help in providing charts, photographs, and historical background.

I'm also grateful to the Beban brothers for their far-out movie and music lists, and Keith Thompson for his wit and wisdom regarding the phenomenal realm of ufology. And special thanks to my friend Sarunas Marciulionis for helping me appreciate the global fascination with UFOs by sharing close encounter reports from his homeland of Lithuania.

Finally, my uforic thanks to Jo Beaton for her help in launching this book, keeping it in orbit, and bringing it safely back down to Earth.

Introduction

The Phenomenon

I was eight years old when I saw my first flying saucer. It was the summer of 1960. I was crouched in the backseat of a spanking new turquoise Nash Rambler with my best friend, Mark Temple, and his younger sister Kim, anxiously staring over the heads of their parents, Val and Wally, at the ominous darkness in front of us.

The night sky seemed to crackle, as if an electrical storm were approaching. A magic cone of flickering white light appeared from a nearby brick building. Suddenly the whole world lit up when a spaceship as wide as a football field *whooshed* across the black vastness of outer space. Slowly, like the words on the stone tablets brought down from the mountain, the movie credits rolled, announcing the phenomenal adventures of *Invaders from Mars*. Fear turned to fascination, anxiety to awe. I was hooked forever.

As best as I can recall, I gained my first heart-swelling glimpse of worlds far beyond our own that night at my hometown's neon-ribboned Wayne Drive-In. In another time and place I might have heard stories about the mythic Celtic fairylands of Tir na Nog, King Arthur's Avalon, or the magic journeys of wayward travelers in old Russia. But this was the America of the 1960s, and the ancient desires for adventure had both accelerated and shifted from the "otherworld" to the stars.

My exploration of those far-flung worlds took off in earnest. Soon I became a science-fiction fanatic, reading all the books on the subject in the school library. Like millions of others, I disappeared into *The Twilight Zone*, ventured into *The Outer Limits*, and reveled at being *Lost in Space*. After watching John Glenn orbit the earth on my family's black-and-white Philco, I was even inspired to cajole Mark and another neighborhood buddy, Steve Shrope, and my brother, Paul, into building our own spaceships out of cardboard refrigerator boxes. With visions of *This Island Earth* and *The Angry Red Planet* flaring in our mind's eye, we spoke to each other via taut string-and-tin can telephone lines, fired death rays from paper towel cannons, and for an entire sweltering summer explored the solar system using maps copied from moldering encyclopedias—without ever leaving our cool Michigan basement. My Uncle Cy, a parachutist during World War II and an avid pilot, was "proud as punch," as he put it, and brought over two fellow pilots from the local hangar to see our "invention." Upon reflection, and after a couple of shots of scotch, he offered to put me and my brother through flight school so we could do more than fantasize.

But not long after our summer of make-believe space travel, the local newspapers began trumpeting what appeared to be a "real flying saucer invasion." On March 14, 1966, farmers and police officers around nearby Ann Arbor reported strange lights hovering over the swampland and highways in the predawn skies. Three nights later, eighty-seven Hillsdale College coeds and their dean watched an astonishing midair acrobatic show as a football-shaped object swayed, wobbled, and glowed in flight for four hours in the distant marshlands. The sightings continued over the next few weeks, the public grew frenzied, and the *Detroit Free Press* ran sensational stories about the goings-on out in Washtenaw County. Finally, to the great relief of embarrassed local officials, an investigator from the now-infamous Project Blue Book team explained that the UFOs were nothing more than "swamp gas" igniting in the marshlands, although this conclusion would later haunt everyone involved.

Looking back, it seems flying saucers were landing everywhere but on the White House lawn, which is exactly where the archskeptics demanded to see them. Rockets, disks, and spaceships adorned magazine covers, emblazoned lunch boxes, and crowned café signs. They bolted across television screens, inspired hit songs, and gave comedians and cartoonists plenty of cosmic material for lampooning a world becoming more lunatic by the hour.

Though reports of heavenly lights date back to the mythical "celestial chariots" of the ancient Hindu epics written circa 500 B.C., what developed through the 1950s and 1960s was an exhilarating belief that the dazzling aerial phenomena might be associated with intelligent life from elsewhere in the universe.

From the legendary sighting of nine strange "skipping objects" over snowcapped Mount Rainier by pilot Kenneth Arnold in that mythic summer of 1947, through the recent spate of reports of aliens visiting unsuspecting souls in the middle of the night, virtually millions of people around the world have experienced something like vindication at the heart of *uforia*, a feeling of being eased or relieved by the indication that a few unsolved mysteries and enigmas remain beyond the scope of calibrators and computers, holding out the possibility of a new vigor and hope.

French ufologist Jacques Vallee gives us a hint of why this might be in his 1979 book *Messengers of Deception*, in which he writes, "Scientific reluctance to consider valid claims of paranormal phenomena is slowly driving many people to accept any claim of superior or mystical contact."

The avid reaction to flying saucer stories and photographs, the fever pitch over rumors of suppressed information about to be released, the undeniable camaraderie exhibited at UFO conventions—all provide moving testimony to Vallee's theory that more people than we may realize believe in, and are experiencing, the *extra*ordinary dimensions of life, experiences that not only science but religion and general opinion are traditionally reluctant to consider authentic.

Uforia is the tumbling blood-rush excitement over the phenomenal sightings experienced around the world this century. It is an echo of deep desire and a fervent hope that "they might be giants," as Cervantes explained Don Quixote's reason for tilting at windmills. In this sense, the strange stories from Mount Rainier, Washington, and Roswell, New Mexico, from Brazil, France, Belgium, and Spain, have cast a spell and helped establish a standard for the coming decades. The UFO phenomenon—a nearly fifty-year pattern of persistent reports of *as yet* unidentified flying objects seen around the world, with discernible patterns or commonalities that don't conform to presently known technologies and cannot be evaluated by the current scientific paradigm—is, as ufologist J. Allen Hynek said, "a matter of fact and not belief."

In fact, people in UFO circles are frequently suspicious of the authoritarian scientific worldview that pretends to explain away so many of the mysteries that imbue life with meaning. Whether or not the UFO phenomenon is revealing that extraterrestrial intelligence is in contact with us here on Earth remains one of the most tantalizing issues of our time. The hundreds of thousands of reports of unexplainable aerial phenomena and otherworldly visitors that have been officially filed since the end of World War II may not have convinced everyone of the existence of physics-defying space travel, much less Close Encounters of the Fourth Kind, but they have accomplished something profound.

For millions of people, the UFO phenomenon, whether experienced firsthand or vicariously through movies, books, or magazines, has reenchanted modern life. Enchantment not in the sense of being hypnotized, but of being deeply moved, revitalized, through a renewed awe and wonder about the riddles of our world.

"Something is being seen," Swiss psychologist Carl Gustav Jung wrote in his 1958 book *Flying Saucers*, "but it isn't known what."

Something, indeed, is in the air. The question from the beginning has been, *what?* Are they *real?* How is it our hearts and minds have been stretched by this tremendous dream from above?

Why us, why now?

A Manual for the Millennium

Perhaps the reader grew up with the specter of flying saucers and alien visitors, or more recently heard tell of the abduction enigma on a television talk show, or read about the parallel universe theory for the origins of UFOs, or laughed uproariously at a *Far Side* cartoon of Stone Age flying saucers built out of giant boulders, or were puzzled by a documentary video "exposing" the UFO "problem" with the "plasma hypothesis," or were intrigued by a recent rash of reports of strange lights in the skies over New Jersey.

If so, maybe you wondered, naturally, what in the devil is going on? What exactly is a UFO? Where do they come from? Why are they here? Am I crazy for believing in them? Who do I turn to if I've had a disturbing experience? Is there a thread that runs from the ancient sightings of shamans and mystics all the way to modern "contacts"? Why have angels, aliens, and UFOs so seized our imagination? Where can I find kindred spirits to share my experiences and theories? Where are the best sites for skywatching? Are there discussion groups, conventions, or on-line forums? Are there *any* reliable answers—or at least intriguing theories—to this enormous riddle?

Since the first wave of saucer sightings hit in the late 1940s, there have been millions more, along with a supporting cast of hundreds of movies, scores of songs, and thousands of books written on the UFO phenomenon. If not the "Event of the Millennium," as trumpeted by researcher Stanton T. Friedman and many others, the prospect that our planet has been monitored, visited, and infiltrated by extraterrestrials has at least triggered one of the biggest publishing phenomena of our time and been a prime supplier of kaleidoscopic images for the Dream Factory of Hollywood.

So while much has been written about the theories of UFOs, aliens, abductions, and other examples of "high strangeness," as Hynek called the most baffling cases, this book offers a simple introduction to many of the mysteries and riddles that comprise the complex phenomenon. Each section includes case studies, reports, and illustrations in an effort to simplify what has become an extremely crowded and confusing field of documentation and debate. There are also sidebars and charts, recommended reading, convention and conference lists, and on-line forums as part of the general survey of this skybreaking phenomenon.

Since there is still no one conclusive answer to any of its vexing aspects, it is hoped that by offering an overview of the UFO field, this book will allow readers to make up their own minds about these riddling questions, especially since the approaching millennium fever is certain to trigger more waves of sightings, and more passionate interest in the exploration of outer space.

Again and again, the UFO question challenges us. It is to many modern explorers what the Sphinx was to ancient travelers: the great riddler, forcing us to reconsider what has been happening in our skies, on our dark country roads, in our bedrooms at 3 A.M.

"Wonderful Things"

When famed archaeologist Howard Carter was asked by fellow explorer Lord Carnarvon if he could see anything as the immense stone door to the four-thousand-year-old crypt of King Tutankhamen was finally wedged open, he peered inside at the "strange animals, statues, and gold—everywhere the glint of gold," and simply said, "Yes . . . wonderful things."

To contemplate the marvelous black-and-white photograph of Carter poised before the royal tomb with a look of rapture on his face and recall the grace of his humble response is to realize what power a revelation can have.

"Wonderful things . . ." that "surpasseth human understanding" are being seen and encountered again by people from every walk of life, from farmers to police officers, people of considerable accomplishment and accountability, from virtually all over the world. Those who haven't experienced similar encounters often find the reports perplexing or literally unbelievable. The paradox of the often unreal atmosphere of the UFO phenomenon is that for many witnesses their experiences and beliefs are exactly what is making life more and more real for them.

Watching, waiting in the long night under the luminous arch of stars and the slow march of planets, some fortunate souls are transported on what the ancients called soul journeys. In their dreamlike narratives, they have the potential to touch the roots of all our lives. As Keith Thompson brilliantly speculated in his imaginative study *Angels and Aliens*, the UFO is perhaps "a key of sorts to the human future," and these sightings may be a hint of the expansion of human perception. If so, the UFO phenomenon might be telling us that while the brain may be satisfied with explanations, the soul requires something else: a quickening of the imagination.

In 1979 Allan Hendry, of the Center for UFO Studies (CUFOS), examined the high percentage of misperceptions of natural phenomena reported via his hot line and concluded that modern culture has drifted further and further from everyday knowledge of nature.

In this light, perhaps we can infer from the UFO phenomenon that we've stopped watching and listening to anything but ourselves, and it is again time to become skywatchers, as the English call lovers of the night sky, and dreamcatchers, the Native American word for those who watch over their nightly soul journeys.

If we can relearn these lost arts as the millennium draws near, we may remember to take the time to sit quietly and pay attention to the strange lights in the dark night. Sometimes those lights move; sometimes they don't. Some may have a mind of their own; some may not.

"Everything is something besides," a poet reminds us. But what? we ask the strange glowing night. And what else?

The First Wave

I observed far to my left and to the north, a formation of very bright objects coming from the vicinity of Mount Baker, flying very close to the mountaintops and traveling at tremendous speed . . .

—Kenneth Arnold, 1947

It was June 24, 1947, only a year before the death of Orville Wright, coinventor, with his brother Wilbur, of the first "flying machine." Kenneth Arnold, a thirty-two-year-old businessman and pilot, was flying his single-engine plane at an altitude of 9,500 feet over the snow-covered Cascade Mountains in Washington state in search of a supposedly downed Marine Corps transport plane, when he saw a blue-white flash in the sky and "a chain of nine peculiar looking aircraft" flying at incredible speed.

"They were approaching Mount Rainier very rapidly, and I merely assumed they were jet planes. Anyhow, I discovered that this was where the reflection had come from, as two or three of them every few seconds would dip or change their course slightly, just enough for the sun to strike them at an angle that reflected brightly on my plane."

The young pilot first thought that there had been a colossal explosion. He glanced at his clock, which read a little before 3 P.M. A few moments later, he witnessed another flash of light and then clearly made out the silvery, crescent-shaped disks, flying diagonally in echelon formation at tremendous speed and skimming across the contours of the mountain. In utter fascination, he tracked them for the next three and a half minutes, especially puzzled by the fact that he couldn't "find any tails on them." Using some quick calculations, he judged their speed to be a staggering 1,656 miles per hour, nearly three times faster

The cover of the debut issue of *Fate* magazine from the spring of 1948, depicting Kenneth Arnold's small plane dwarfed by stylized "flying disks" and announcing the scoop of the decade: Arnold's first-person account.

than any jet currently in operation. As an experienced pilot, he realized these peculiar craft defied any technology he knew of, and he said as much when he landed at Yakima around 4 P.M. After Arnold regaled his friends with the story, one fellow pilot declared the objects to be a "salvo of guided missiles from a nearby test range," but even he couldn't imagine for the life of him how missiles could bank and turn so sharply.

By the time he landed in Pendleton, Oregon, reporters were avidly waiting for him. His unassailable stature in the community ensured both a large turnout and questions more respectful than usual under the circumstances. When asked to describe the strange disks, he struggled to form the right image. Speedboats in rough water, he ventured, then he described them as being like the swooping tail of a Chinese kite.

Finally Arnold said, "They flew like a saucer would if you skipped it across the water." Going on, he described the objects as flying over the mountains like geese in a diagonal formation, as well as "flat like a pie pan and so shiny that they reflected the sun like a mirror." Clearly, he was an unusually descriptive flier, or was so affected by his afternoon flight that the images wouldn't stop coming. Either way, the next day one

Photo courtesy of the Library of Congress

Kenneth Arnold, whose sighting of nine mysterious objects over Mount Rainier in 1947 virtually launched the modern UFO craze.

12

of his colorful metaphors made headlines, with a little help from the local scribes.

Bill Bequette, a reporter who had been scribbling down the story as fast as he heard it, latched onto the word "saucer," and so was coined a phrase known the world over: flying saucer. It's an origin story that dictionary hounds from Dr. Johnson to William Safire would love, but the image behind it has proven to be more than another piece of literary trivia. The very shape insinuated by the word "saucer" would help form, in a mysterious manner, what people saw and how they expressed their visions for the next five decades. The expression compressed numerous sightings into one distinct image that would stand in for an ever-changing kaleidoscope of images of electrifying aerial phenomena.

The headlines of the next day's *Seattle Post-Intelligencer* announced: "Mystery Disks Hurtling Across the Sky." The Cascades incident sparked debate, conversation, satire, and imaginations everywhere. At first, critics didn't dare attack a rescue pilot and firefighting-equipment salesman as a hoaxer or crank, so their dubiousness centered on his forgivable misjudgment of distance. The military characteristically dismissed the sighting as an optical illusion, a mountain mirage. The *New York Times* suggested he saw nothing more than "atoms escaping from an overwrought bomb." Daniel Cohen's version of the epochal event was that Arnold "may have seen clouds created by wind currents from the mountains, or an optical illusion resulting from unusual meteorological conditions."

> *Finally Arnold said, "They flew like a saucer would if you skipped it across the water." Bill Bequette, a reporter who had been scribbling down the story as fast as he heard it, latched onto the word "saucer," and so was coined a phrase known the world over: flying saucer.*

Arnold was famous for only slightly longer than the requisite fifteen minutes. Not long after his story rippled around the globe the naysayers, cynics, debunkers, and other skeptics began to satirize the young pilot's claim. They accused him of borrowing the image of otherworldly flying machines from science-fiction works he must have recently read, such as *The War of the Worlds*, H. G. Wells's tall tale of Martian invaders cosmically catapulted to Earth.

Although he was quoted soon after the incident as saying, "I thought it wouldn't be long before there was one of these things in every garage," Arnold eventually admitted he regretted going public with his sighting, claiming he wouldn't report a "flying ten-story building" after the way he was treated by the debunking press and a skeptical public.

Yet not even the early skeptics knew what to make of the fact that the same day as Arnold's sighting there were at least eighteen others in the Pacific Northwest, and within the next few days at least another twenty sightings of similar unidentifiable objects. During the week of July 5, 100 reports a day were filed and by the end of 1947, 850 sightings had been reported around the country. An American historian of the period wrote: "The floodgates were now open for the rush of reports that was soon to follow. But it had taken a man of Arnold's character and forthright conviction to open them."

In the six months that followed, Air Force researchers found 156 reports worthy of further study. True-blue believers and the newly converted found cosmic, overarching meaning in every report. Skeptics discounted them as common misperceptions, and the military downplayed the incidents in public while thoroughly investigating them in private, worried that the strange streaking objects might be secret Soviet weapons. By the end of 1947, Lieutenant General Nathan F. Twining, the commanding officer at Wright Field (later renamed Wright Patterson Air Force Base), would notify the Pentagon: "The phenomenon reported is something real and not visionary or fictitious."

Washington was impressed enough to found Project Sign, issuing orders to collect and evaluate "all information concerning sightings and phenomena in the atmosphere which can be construed to be of concern to the national security."

Over the next five years, thousands of sightings of unidentified flying objects would be reported, some in terror, some in passing interest—others part of elaborate hoaxes. They came in waves, hundreds in a month. Moviegoers across the country watched cheesy newsreels, such as "Nation Stirred by Mystery of Discs in the Sky," narrated by the famous world traveler and voice of a thousand documentaries, Lowell Thomas himself.

Sightings occurred in forty states and several foreign countries. With memories of secret rockets still fresh from World War II, the U.S. Army dispatched planes with mounted cameras to patrol the skies for flying saucers.

The Skies Would Never Be the Same Again

Gradually, the novelty of the Arnold incident wore off, and newspapers and the radio began labeling every claim a hoax filed by a moonstruck crackpot. "Let anyone breathe the word 'saucer,' and up

Colonel L. Gordon Cooper, one of the original Mercury 7 astronauts, claims to have chased a UFO in 1951 while he was a fighter pilot in Germany. In a letter sent to the United Nations in 1978 to express his views on UFOs, he stated: "I believe that these extraterrestrial vehicles and their crews are visiting this planet from other planets which obviously are a little more technically advanced than we are here on earth."

will pop some citizen who might even claim to have ridden in a weird space vehicle, steered by little green men with pink eyes, who conversed fluently in pig-Latin," John Godwin wrote of the time in *This Baffling World*.

Regardless of what Kenneth Arnold did or did not see, and despite the ridicule of the media and government cover-ups, the genie was out of the bottle. The "modern flying saucer era" had begun, and the skies would never be the same again.

Arnold's sighting wasn't the first of its kind, but it accomplished what all great mythic acts do by constellating the hopes and aspirations, the fears and anxieties of an entire age, and by crystallizing in a single image what appears to be the end of one era—and the beginning of another.

While belief in celestial powers is ancient and universal, the age of space travel has revitalized the idea and imagery of supernatural beings intruding into and influencing human existence. Like the symbol of the hovering "Eye of God" reported in the skies of medieval Europe, the rash of sightings that followed Kenneth Arnold's is uncannily reminiscent of the ancient suspicion that the world was being "watched," if not invaded, from above.

A great cultural controversy to rival anything in the "angels dancing on a pinhead" style of debate of the Middle Ages had begun. The waves of saucer sightings would soon be called an "epidemic" and, only slightly more benevolently, "discomania." Early debunkers compared "saucer madness" to the long history of "mass delusion" in medieval Europe's intrigue with the paranormal—from devils, ghosts, witches, and werewolves to leprechauns, trolls, and fairies—dubbed by nineteenth-century author Charles Langley as "extraordinary popular delusions and the madness of crowds."

But as UFO researcher Jenny Randles has pointed out, the difference between the Great Airship Mystery of 1896 and the Flying Saucer Phenomenon of 1947 was confidence in what was being seen. The wild assortment of "heavier-than-air" flying machines that thousands saw at the turn of the century were assumed to be simply proof of the famous American ingenuity, such was the confidence in Yankee know-how at the time, combined with a growing familiarity with fantastic travel as vividly described in early science-fiction stories. But the Arnold incident drew such inflamed denials from the government and such scorn from the scientific community that after all the press conferences nobody could be sure what was going on in the skies above.

The eminent astronomer Dr. C. C. Wylie suggested at the 1947 gathering of the American Association for the Advancement of Science that the reason behind the national hysteria over UFOs was "the present failure of scientific men to explain promptly and accurately flaming objects seen over several states, flying saucers, and other celestial phenomena which arouse national interest."

Aviation pioneer Orville Wright was also suspicious. Interviewed shortly after Arnold's sighting, he seemed embittered by the specter of what his "flying machine" had been transformed into, declaring, "It is more propaganda for war to stir up the people and to excite them to believe a foreign power has designs on this nation."

As America drifted into the Cold War, those fears would be ignited again and again, and were vividly portrayed in a spate of science-fiction "invasion" films. But in the first Gallup Poll on the "Flying Saucer" question, conducted in August 1947, two months after Arnold's sighting, UFOs registered a phenomenal 90 percent awareness rate (one of the highest ever recorded) and showed, at least for the time being, how most people figured that the mystery objects were optical illusions or secret weapons gone astray. Few would make the connection of flying disks and extraterrestrial intelligence for another several years.

But already the great riddle had been posed. Depending on your sources and your belief system, we were either in great trouble—or greatly troubled.

Incident at Roswell

"Well, how in the hell does a weather balloon affect national security?"
> —from the movie *Roswell: The UFO Cover-up*

The clamor over the Mount Rainier sighting had barely subsided when another skyquake was felt a couple of weeks later, this time in New Mexico. On the night of July 2, a sheep rancher named Mac Brazel heard a tremendous explosion louder than the thunderclaps of that night's violent storm. The following morning he ventured out over the Foster Ranch near Corona and found pieces of "the strangest stuff" he'd ever seen, as he later told Floyd Proctor, his nearest neighbor. The metal-like material that was strewn over a three-quarter-mile area was as light and thin as tinfoil, but witnesses later claimed you couldn't dent it with a sledgehammer or cut it with a knife. When crumpled, it would pop back to its original shape. In addition, there were I-beam pieces that were as light as balsa wood and etched with indecipherable pastel-colored hieroglyphics, which Brazel described as looking like the figures on firecracker wrappers.

Several days later, Brazel was having a few beers at the tavern in Corona, when he heard about recent flying saucer sightings and a $3,000 reward for proof of "flying disks." Thinking he might have stumbled across something important, he informed the local sheriff's department, which in turn

> *"UFOs have brought about a unique situation: hundreds of thousands of people claim to have seen something which hundreds of thousands of other people insist do not exist."*
>
> —John Godwin, *This Baffling World*

contacted the intelligence office of the Eighth Air Force at Roswell Army Air Field. Mystified, base intelligence officer Major Jesse A. Marcel drove out to the debris site with a counterintelligence officer, Captain Sheridan Cavitt, and gathered as much of the material as he could fit into his military jeep and returned across seventy-five miles of desolate desert. He arrived home late at night and showed pieces of the peculiar debris to his wife and son. The next morning, he returned to his post at the nearby airfield, which until that moment had been most famous for its 509th Bomb Group, which had dropped the atomic bombs on Japan at the end of World War II.

The ensuing official military press release by public information officer Lieutenant Walter Haut claimed that the remnants of a crashed "flying disk" had been discovered outside Roswell. The phones at the local police station and the *Roswell Daily Record* lit up with calls from curious newspaper reporters from Sacramento to London asking if the preposterous rumor was true: had the U.S. Army discovered a crashed flying saucer in New Mexico?

On July 8, the *Roswell Daily Record* published Haut's press release and was taken off the wire for publication by other evening papers across the country:

> The many rumors regarding the flying disk became a reality yesterday when the intelligence office of the 509th Bomb Group of the Eighth Air Force, Roswell Army Air Field, was fortunate enough to gain possession of a disk through the cooperation of one of the local ranchers and the sheriff's office of Chaves County.

The perplexing fragments were flown to Eighth Air Force headquarters in Fort Worth, Texas, then on to Wright Field in Dayton, Ohio, for further analysis. By this time, the authorities were in a panic.

Gallup Poll

Q

Have you heard or read about "flying saucers"?

	July 25–30, 1947	May 1–5, 1960
Yes	90%	94%
No	10%	6%

Q

Asked of those who answered yes, what do you think these flying saucers are?

1947

Optical illusion, imagination	.29%
A hoax	.10%
U.S. secret weapon	.15%
Weather forecasting devices	.3%
Russian secret weapon	.1%
Airplane searchlights	.2%
Other answers, don't know	.42%

1960

Optical illusion, pipe dreams, hoax, etc.	.16%
Army or navy experiments, new weapon, military secret	.23%
Weather forecasting devices	.4%
Russian secret weapon	.3%
Some kind of new airplane	.6%
Comets, shooting stars, something from another planet	.5%
No such thing	.6%
Other answers, don't know	.32%

Source: The Gallup Organization (U.S.A.)

Before actually seeing any of the disputed material, Brigadier General Roger Ramey called the original announcement a mistake. He claimed the recovered debris was simply the wreckage of an experimental weather device. He immediately ordered Marcel to Fort Worth for a briefing. At an Air Force press conference held the evening of July 8, Marcel was staggered by the official order to keep silent and pose for newspaper photographs while holding the pieces of a weather balloon that had been substituted for the material he had personally delivered to the base at Roswell. Later, he and everyone else involved in the seizing of the mystery wreckage were ordered to maintain a lifelong silence for the sake of national security.

As quickly as the furor over the rumor of a crashed saucer had lit up switchboards and imaginations, it died down. The case was officially closed. Some people believed that the debris was fragments

Photo courtesy of the *Roswell Daily Record*

of errant missiles from the nearby White Sands base or remnants of a secret weapon from Los Alamos. Others took the government at its word that a new-fangled weather balloon had gone astray, an explanation revived forty-seven years later. In September 1994 the Air Force finally responded to the niggling Roswell question by attributing the whole incident to a certain Project Mogul, which was testing top secret weather balloons designed to detect Russian satellites.

Then and now, there are many who have wondered why an errant weather balloon could threaten the security of what was being touted as the strongest nation on earth.

Ever since the inauspicious press conference on the Roswell incident in the late summer of 1947, the debate between the government and the public over UFOs has been fractious. There has been the official position that UFOs are either unidentified lights, flashes, and streaks in the sky or "hoaxes, erroneously identified friendly objects, meteorological phenomenon or light aberrations," as one military spokesman concluded. On the other hand, there are thousands of witnesses and believers who insist their sightings and experiences are real and cannot be explained away as dismissively as a nightmare to a child.

Inside the gap between these two competing realities grew a powerful legend: the wreckage of an actual flying saucer had indeed been taken to Wright Field, along with the bodies of five aliens, one of whom was still alive and communicated telepathically with its captors.

Off-course flying saucers from distant worlds zapped in a lightning storm crash in the desert? A top secret weapon accidentally detonated? An experimental weather balloon? No one knows for sure what came down in Roswell in the summer of 1947, but the incident has become the most scrutinized, the most debated, the most visible case in the annals of UFO studies.

An uneasy silence has reigned over the incident for the last fifty years, amid tremendous resentment from the families of those involved, silent because their lives were threatened, according to many survivors. It was not to be investigated again until the mid-1970s when authors Charles Berlitz and William Moore began research for their book, *The Roswell Incident*. In 1978, when the still-haunted Jesse Marcel was interviewed by Stanton T. Friedman, and again for a subsequent television program, he declared that the debris he found "was something I had never seen before or since . . . it certainly wasn't anything built by us."

Regardless of the official cover-up, the debate was about to begin again in earnest. *Something* had happened at Roswell that has come to symbolize what we don't yet know about the nature of life on other planets, the possibility of intergalactic travel, the state of national security and how far the government will go to ensure it. It was our *desire*, as psychologist Carl Jung would describe it eleven years later in his book on flying saucers and the mythic imagination, to believe in mysteries that stir the soul.

"According to Donald Keyhoe, in his book, The Flying Saucers Are Real, *the word 'saucer' was first used in this context in the* Denison Daily News *of 25th January, 1878. A Mr. John Martin, a farmer living near Denison, Texas, was reported as having seen a dark object high in the southern sky. He describes the wonderful speed with which it flew and when it came directly overhead 'it was about the size of a large saucer and was evidently at a great height.' The newspaper concluded the account by describing Mr. Martin as a gentleman of undoubted veracity 'and this strange occurrence, if it was not a balloon, deserves the attention of our scientists.'"*

—Waveney Girvan, *Flying Saucers and Common Sense*

Whatever happened at Roswell has become a mirror for what we think about the meaning of life, the secret dealings of the military, the nature of phenomena, and the mysteries of the night sky. We are forced to consider the implications for our religious, social, political, and military institutions if it were to suddenly and irrevocably be proven that *we are not alone*.

The Ripples of the Wave

In the months after the Kenneth Arnold encounter and the Roswell incident, a wave of sightings rippled out across the world. On June 26, only two days after Arnold's experience, it was reported in the Associated Press that W. I. Davenport, a carpenter, sighted "nine shiny objects flying at a high rate of speed" in Arnold's hometown of Boise, Idaho. A private pilot named Vernon Baird reported knocking a "pearl gray, clam-shaped" craft resembling a yo-yo out of the sky over Montana. As Keith Thompson vividly describes it, "The story is carried by newspapers throughout the nation. In a one-paragraph report the following day, Baird admits he fabricated the story while shooting the breeze with other pilots around the hangar. He promises not to do it again."

The French scientist Jacques Vallee discovered another incident from that period in Bauru, near Pitanga, Brazil, of a hissing, flying disk terrifying a surveyors' group. Jose C. Higgins reported that three tall beings in translucent suits, with oversize heads and huge round eyes, disembarked and drew a map of the solar system to show that they came from Uranus.

In May 1948 Captain C. S. Chiles, a veteran Eastern Airlines pilot, and copilot John Whitted encountered a 100-foot-long, cigar-shaped, wingless aircraft while

> "*I must insist upon full access to discs recovered. . . . The Army grabbed one and would not let us have it for cursory examination.*"
> —J. Edgar Hoover, Director, FBI, 1947

flying their DC-3 between Montgomery and Mobile, Alabama. Chiles reported, "Whatever it was it flashed down toward us, and we veered off to the left. It veered to its left and passed up about 700 feet to our right and a little above us. Then, as if the pilot had seen us and wanted to avoid us, it pulled up with a tremendous burst of flame from the rear, and zoomed into the clouds, its prop wash or jet wash rocking our plane."

In France, Alain Berard reported seeing a bright green lightning flash after which a large, bright object landed near his farm. Upon approach he saw three stocky, headless figures. Terrified, he shot at the aliens, and the object flew away—vertically.

An unpredictable mix of authentic, alarmed, and hoax sightings occurred until the next critical UFO episode took place. On the afternoon of July 7, 1948, state police in Madisonville, Kentucky, spotted an enormous UFO heading straight toward Goodman Air Force Base. The warning was relayed to Colonel Guy Hix, commanding officer. Four minutes later, Colonel Hix, along with five officers and an aide,

> *"That Saucer You Saw, Sir!"*
> —headline in the
> *Irish Times,*1951

watched the "conelike" metallic object, its top glowing a crimson-yellow, hover over the airfield. Hix ordered three F-51 fighter planes to scramble in pursuit, led by Captain Thomas Mantell. Within minutes, Mantell claimed he had "that thing" directly in front, then said, "I'm at 10,000 feet and pursuing it. It's going up and forward now as fast as I am—that's 360 mph. I'll pursue it as high as 20,000 feet." Those were his famous last words. The other two craft returned to the base as the disk climbed upward, but Mantell continued his pursuit.

The wreckage of his plane was found strewn over a three-mile area later that afternoon. The initial Air Force verdict was that Mantell had died while chasing the light of the planet Venus, but the rumor was that he had mistaken the flash for a flying saucer. Eventually, declassified documents revealed that secret Navy reconnaissance Skyhook balloons were being tested in the area. After an eighteen-month investigation, the official explanation came down: "Captain Mantell had probably blacked out at 20,000 feet from lack of oxygen." Mantell became the first martyr in the annals of ufology, and a legend grew that a brave pilot had been shot down by a UFO and the military was hiding the truth.

Who Sees What?

Though still considered saucer-shaped in the public's mind and mythology, UFOs have been seen in every shape and size imaginable, a veritable kaleidoscope of ever-changing appearances. They can be as small as pinpricks or as large as buildings, or might appear as spots of light that dance in curlicuing patterns across the sky.

There are nocturnal lights, known as NLs, and daytime sightings, nicknamed DDs, for daylight discs. UFOs have been reported to be shaped like boomerangs, spheres, diamonds, cigars, ironing boards, flat disks, inverted or partially melted ice cream cones, and triangles. They've been playfully described as "skyborne somethings," "hovering zooming whatzits," "magnetic flutterings," "a piece of crockery," and "machines splitting the sky"—yet are also dismissed contemptuously as mere "will-o'-the-wisps," "friar's lanterns," "jack-o'-lanterns," "sunspots," "fireflies on windscreens," "personal illusions" and "mass delusions," "summer sickness," and "inspired" and "insidious hoaxes."

UFOs have been seen traveling alone, in pairs, and occasionally in large groups; as onetime appearances and in "rashes" or "flaps," detectable patterns of sightings. They've been reported to fly in and out again, like tour buses visiting famous European ruins for an hour then moving on, but also have been seen

26

How to Define

UFO Classifications

Nocturnal Lights

NL

These are sightings of well-defined lights in the night sky whose appearance and/or motion are not explainable in terms of conventional light sources. The light appears most often as red, blue, orange, or white. They form the largest group of UFO reports.

Daylight Discs

DD

Daytime sightings are generally of oval or disk-shaped, metallic-appearing objects. They can appear high in the sky or close to the ground, and they are often reported to hover. They can seem to disappear with astounding speed.

Radar-Visual

RV

Of special significance are unidentified "blips" on radar screens that coincide with and confirm simultaneous visual sightings by the same or other witnesses. These cases are infrequent.

UFO Sightings

Relatively Close Sightings
(within 200 yards)

Close Encounters of the First Kind
Though the witness observes a UFO nearby, there appears to be no interaction with either the witness or the environment.

CE1

Close Encounters of the Second Kind
These encounters include details of interaction between the UFO and the environment, which may vary from interference with car ignition systems and electronic gear to imprints or burns on the ground and physical effects on plants, animals, and humans.

CE2

Close Encounters of the Third Kind
Occupants of a UFO—entities that are humanlike ("humanoid") or not humanlike—have been reported. There is usually no direct contact or communication with the witness.

CE3

Close Encounters of the Fourth Kind
Onboard experiences or abductions of individuals or people, usually in the presence of humanoids. This classification was added recently, as reports of incidents involving very close contact—even detainment of witnesses—have increased.

CE4

This classification system was developed by J. Allen Hynek of the Center for UFO Studies. Used with permission of CUFOS.

suctioning up animals with their death rays, or landing in cornfields and leaving behind marvelous geometric patterns on the ground. They've even been spotted flying like flocks of geese over drive-in movie screens.

The *disc*ussion flourishes. Since Kenneth Arnold's wild saucer chase in 1947, the sky has never looked quite the same. While the eyes of the world's many curious souls turn to the heavens with each announcement of a NASA space shuttle launch, a chance passing of a comet, or a solar or lunar eclipse, the *unexplainable* aerial phenomenon continues to dazzle those who fervently believe there are wonders unfolding all around us that are beyond the reaches of modern technology.

Despite various attempts by the government, media, and academia to convince the public otherwise, UFOs are still an intriguing enigma to the millions who believe they have encountered the *presence* of something that changed their lives forever.

As psychologist Michael Grosso has written, these are "experiences that shatter people's sense of reality," sightings that have affected people every bit as powerfully as glimpses of classical gods or medieval saints moved people of previous eras. On the shadow side of the phenomena, encounters have often left witnesses with a type of post-traumatic stress syndrome, according to psychologists who worked with abductees.

> *"Something is being seen, but it isn't known what. . . . This formulation leaves the question of 'seeing' open. Something material could be seen, or something psychic could be seen. Both are realities, but of different kinds."*
>
> —Carl Gustav Jung,
> *Flying Saucers*

Hard Objects

Variation on a much-heralded UFO chart published for the hearings before the House Committee on Space and Astronautics in 1968. Each drawing was modeled after a UFO reported in an actual case.

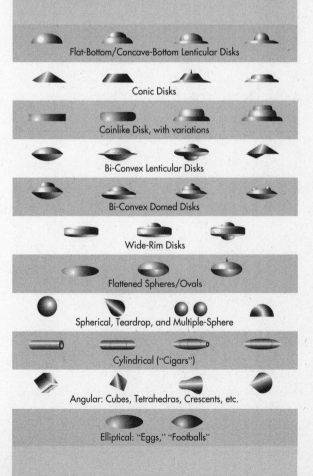

Flat-Bottom/Concave-Bottom Lenticular Disks

Conic Disks

Coinlike Disk, with variations

Bi-Convex Lenticular Disks

Bi-Convex Domed Disks

Wide-Rim Disks

Flattened Spheres/Ovals

Spherical, Teardrop, and Multiple-Sphere

Cylindrical ("Cigars")

Angular: Cubes, Tetrahedras, Crescents, etc.

Elliptical: "Eggs," "Footballs"

Perhaps UFOs are signs of a new era, "heralds of a changing of the gods," as Jung regarded them. Or perhaps they are the result of natural deceptions? Phosphenes or stars in the eyes? Kundalini heat visions? Spikes of lights? Gargoyles in the sky? There are several current theories vying for the elusive "one explanation" that will tie in the many facets of the phenomenon. As time marches on the debate has only intensified.

Book Guide

**Flying Saucers: A Modern Myth of
Things Seen in the Sky**
Carl Gustav Jung (Princeton University Press, 1978)

The Roswell Incident
Charles Berlitz and William L. Moore
(Berkley Books, 1988)

The UFO Controversy in America
David M. Jacobs
(Indiana University Press, 1975)

UFO Crash at Roswell
Kevin D. Randle and Donald R. Schmitt
(Avon Books, 1991)

The UFO Experience
J. Allen Hynek
(Corgi, 1972)

Ancient Skywatching:

From Flying Dragons to Ghost Rockets

Look at the stars! Look up at the skies!
O look at all the fire-folk sitting in the air!
The bright boroughs, the circle-citadels there!
          —Horace, Roman poet, first century B.C.

For thousands of years people have been fascinated by the weird and wonderful phenomena of mysterious lights and unidentified figures flashing across the sky. The unexplained energies of nature are at the root of many of our most colorful legends and myths of the heavens. The ancients called them "strange prodigies," "angels," "gods," "celestial chariots," "golden globes," "night suns," "burning shields," and myriad other poetic names.

One of the first recorded baffling sightings appears in an ancient Indian architectural text and guide to city planning, the *Samarangana-Sartradhara*, from the fifth century B.C., which contained a report of *vimana*s, deadly machines that were flown by pilots. Similar vehicles are described in the Hindu epics, the *Mahabharata* and *Ramayana*, as phenomenal flying war machines. An ancient Chinese legend describes a distant "land of flying carts" inhabited by one-armed, three-eyed people piloting winged chariots with gold wheels. In 329 B.C. Alexander the Great's army was repeatedly attacked from the sky by two unidentified flying "silver shields."

"The Spiritual Pilgrim," adapted by the French astronomer Camille Flammarion from a sixteenth-century German woodcut.

Skyborne curiosities are later referred to by the Romans as "phantom chariots." Livy wrote of an object resembling a flying altar in the sky at Hadria in Italy in 214 B.C. Pliny the Elder described "gleaming beams in the sky" and how one "spark" the size of the moon fell to earth before inexplicably rising back into the heavens.

Even the Bible contains a famous passage that has tantalized UFO enthusiasts: that of Ezekiel's enigmatic vision of "whirlwinds" that manifested in "a wheel in the middle of a wheel." It fired "lightning" bolts as it descended, churning up the desert sands, from which emerged four winged beings.

From the visions of New Jerusalem to Gulliver's vision of the flying city of Laputa, entire communities have been observed in the heavens. Charles Fort, the "connoisseur of phenomena," collected such reports from the last several centuries. Among them are clever accounts of phantom islands: a "distant land with wonderful white buildings" seen off the coast of the Orkney Islands in 1840; "an extensive ancient city abounding with the ruins of castles, obelisks, churches and monuments" sighted off the shores of West Greenland in 1820; and a phantom city of futuristic architectural designs off the seaweed-strewn sands of Ballyconneely, Connemara, in Ireland's rugged west, on view for three hours on August 2, 1908.

> "The belief in Beings from the skies who surveyed our Earth persisted in human consciousness throughout the Middle Ages."
> —W. R. Drake,
> *Spacemen in the Middle Ages*

A much published broadsheet of an aerial war over the German city of Nuremberg on April 4, 1561, looks like the medieval equivalent of a poster for the science-fiction movie *Invaders from Mars*. Strange objects are seen hurtling through the air, as "the sky was filled with cylindrical shapes from which emerged black, red, orange and blue-white spheres that darted about." It was, they said, "a very

Flying Dragons

During the Middle Ages, unidentified flying dragons were the scourge of Europe. For centuries, the lightning-eyed, fire-breathing, pearl-foreheaded dragons that hid in clouds and caves were the bane of the Church and the overly pious. Valiant heroes were sent on quests to rid the land and sky of the pagan beasts.

As late as the thirteenth century, the citizens of London were still reporting flying dragons and using alarmed language not unlike that evoked by the 1952 "flying saucer scare" in Washington D.C. Of course, we haven't strayed that far from our own infatuation with dragons. Seven centuries later, we are still watched over by celestial serpents in the form of the constellations Cetus and Draco the Dragon, and they continue to entrance us in fantasy books and games such as Dungeons and Dragons.

Adaptation of a medieval IFO (identified flying object), a flying dragon of the variety reported in the skies of Europe as late as the seventeenth century.

frightful spectacle" observed by "numerous men and women," in which the spheres, crosses, and tubes fought with each other for an hour until they fell to the earth in a cloud of steam before lifting off and fading away. Naturally, the terrifying celestial display was interpreted as a warning for people to end their sinful ways, just as the denizens of today's UFOs are often reported to deliver apocalyptic messages about the consequences of our own misbehavior.

Five years later, Samuel Coccius, a student in Basel, Switzerland, reported "many large, black globes were seen in the air, moving before the sun at great speed and turning against each other as if fighting. Some of them became red and fiery and afterwards faded and went out." In 1606 fireballs seen over Nijo castle in Kyoto were described by witnesses as spinning wildly like a red wheel. Centuries later, in 1893, the strange globular, reddish "Japanese Lights" often reappeared in groups on cold, clear nights, resembling, it was said, Chinese lanterns drifting in the sky.

Medieval illustration from the *Basel Broadsheet* depicting the celestial fireball and black globe display witnessed by hundreds over Basel, Switzerland, on August 7, 1566.

The Great American Airship Scare

During the nineteenth century, science and technology revolutionized not only how people lived but how they imagined the world—and the future—to be. In Zacatecas, Mexico, José Bonilla, the director of an observatory, was photographing sunspots when he noticed odd glowing objects racing across the face of the sun. In a paper published for the astronomical community, he wrote: "I was able to fix their trajectory across the solar disk . . . some appeared round or spherical, but one notes in the photographs that the bodies are not spherical but irregular in form. Before crossing the solar disk these bodies threw out brilliant trains of light but in crossing the sun they seemed to become opaque and dark against its brighter background." To back up his claim, he snapped what some observers, including Jenny Randles, Director of Investigations for BUFORA (British UFO Research Association), believe to be the first photograph of a UFO: a hazy shot of the sun with a "five-pointed star with dark center." The year was 1883.

In 1886 the prolific French author and visionary Jules Verne published his thirty-first book, *Robur the Conqueror*, an adventure story with a plotline that could pass for a UFO "flap" today. An unexplainable object is sighted in the sky all over the world, accompanied by bizarre lights and sounds, and aerial flashes. A vapor cloud by day, at night it's a silhouette. As it turns out, the phantom object is a flying machine, the ominously named *Albatross*, created by Robur, who even abducts three unsuspecting souls for an around-the-world flight. Verne's relationship to the UFO phenomenon is an intriguing one because of his immense influence on English and American "interplanetary fiction," dime novels of the 1880s and 1890s that revolved around airships. Thousands of copies of dime novels about flying machines were in circulation by the end of the century, stories vaunting the new age of "heavier-than-air" flight—machine flight.

In November 1896 a strange oblong or cigar-shaped craft driven by whirling propellers and featuring powerful searchlights was spotted in the night sky over Sacramento, California. It was nicknamed the "California Great Airship." Within days the "wandering apparition," as one newspaper described it, was sighted in Oakland and San Francisco, where it scared the seals off their rocks! The sightings—by earnest people who vigorously denied that the craft were either balloons or gliders—continued until the following April, and were reported over the Great Lakes, Texas, and the Great Plains. Witnesses described strange dirigible-shaped airships with blazing searchlights floating over farmland and cities. From some, it was told, came "sweet strains of music." Other accounts tell of egg-shaped or barrel-shaped airships, even a thirty-foot canoe, as was reported floating over Kansas, or an airship with flapping wings. There are also innumerable accounts of the landings of huge craft whose pilots spoke in perfect English to the startled witnesses on the ground.

Things got curiouser and curiouser. On April 19, 1897, cattle rancher Alexander Hamilton, along with his son and a hired man, was startled to see a 300-foot-long cigar-shaped airship with "panels of glass or other transparent substance," whose occupants were "six of the strangest beings I ever saw," lower a red cable and fasten it around one of his heifers. They watched "in amazement to see ship, cow and all, rise slowly and sail off." The papers that dared carry the story the next day included printed affidavits from prominent local citizens. Though later exposed as a hoax by Hamilton, who belonged to the local "liar's club," a popular organization in an era of the tall tale, knee-slapping brand of humor, the story is still fascinating for revealing the kind of images that were considered believable at the time.

Many investigators of the day scoffed at the airship appearances as mere hoaxes or sensational stories concocted by yellow journalists to exploit some current ideas about Martian canals and extraterrestrial life gleaned from the fantastic science-fiction stories of Verne and H. G. Wells.

Although it now appears, as Ron Miller has discussed in an intriguing article that appeared in the May/June 1987 issue of *Journal of UFO Studies*, that the mass sightings were probably influenced by the rage for Jules Verne-style aerial adventure tales, the vivid accounts still mark history's first documented UFO reports, as they remained unidentified at a time when folks were not yet jaded to out-of-this-world stories. Not unlike the dragon sightings in cultures that reveled in telling dragon stories around the hearth, the airships that set hearts racing at the turn of the century resembled the flying machines, dirigibles, and ornithopters that the world was beginning to accept to be as real as the sky and the stars. By then, the age of technology was in full flight, as was the American Dream.

Anything that could be imagined was.

> *The godfather of rocketry, Wernher von Braun, has been quoted as saying about extraterrestrials, "It is as impossible to confirm them in the present as it will be to deny them in the future."*

The Foo Fighters

Since the "flap" of 1896, there's been no lack of spectacular and flabbergasting flying objects in our skies. World War II pilots from several countries reported strange glowing balls of light darting around their airplanes. Nicknamed "foo fighters," after a nonsense phrase used by a cartoon character by the name of Smokey Stover, "Where there's foo there's fire" (apparently a corruption of the French word *feu*, for fire), the lights were at first assumed to be St. Elmo's Fire, electrical discharges that are often seen on wingtips or the mastheads of ships. But as the reports piled up so did the anxiety that the lights were hostile, though they never exacted any damage. The Allies figured the incredible lights were wispy evidence of German surveillance devices or radar scramblers, even secret weapons of psychological warfare. By war's end they discovered that the German and Japanese pilots had also been tailed by the strange lights and had believed them to be of American or British origin.

After the war, U.S. Army experts concluded that the foo fighters were nothing but "mass hallucinations." To the public this was disturbing, if not preposterous, since the reports were coming from the very pilots who were supposed to be the most reliable, eagle-eyed fliers in the world.

The freaky foo phenomenon continued on into the Korean and Vietnam wars, splitting the debate about UFOs into the usual two camps: some ufologists considered the apparitions to be proof of time-and-space defying extraterrestrial visitors, while the debunkers stoically explained the lights as ordinary manifestations of ball lightning zipping around the fighter planes, or ice crystal reflections in the cockpit.

Rare photograph taken over Germany in 1944 of the mysterious "foo fighters," which perplexed Allied and Axis pilots in World War II but never caused any harm. Similar sightings were reported in the Korean and Vietnam conflicts.

The Winged

Since the time of the ancient Egyptians, over thirty-four centuries ago, people have imagined the world to be animated by mighty eyelike configurations in the sky. For some, it was the solar eye of a distant god, or the eye of a flying dragon. For certain Eskimo cultures the sun was a door through which shamans passed to earn immortality. To the ancient Egyptians the winged eye was symbolic of divine omniscience and power, yet at the same time was seen as a flaming sign of destruction. The most fiery ray of the sun, Francis Huxley points out, "can overcome the visual ray and penetrate eyeballs, causing them to water and confuse the spectrum of color which [Plato] called 'the dazzling.'" Elsewhere, the eye has been symbolic of initiation

Eye in the Sky

into the mysteries, an emblem of the contemplation of infinity, or the place where love is born.

In the Mediterranean and parts of Africa, a glass or clay evil eye has long represented "the searching eye of sovereignty," reflective of cultures laboring under intense supervision and oppression, often to the point of paranoia. In our time, the fear of the evil eye was vividly illustrated by George Orwell's "universal television camera," which follows people everywhere in his prescient book *1984*, and surrealists from De Chirico to Magritte painted "eyes in the skies" spying on unsuspecting souls.

Likewise, the annals of ufology are riddled with reports of "sightings" of lights in the sky, usually oval, often lenticular (lens-shaped), which, with intriguing consistency, are described as watching, observing, following the contactees. In a way, they echo ancient teaching stories of the "Open Eye," the eye of "Higher" perception, the one that reminds us the Eye of God is upon us, an invocation to open our eyes.

The floating "Eye of God" (left), symbol of the divine and omniscient presence in feudal life. It is evocative of the classic saucer shapes (above) often uncannily reported as "watching over" startled witnesses and observers.

Ghost Rockets over Scandinavia

In 1946, the year after World War II ended, newspapers across Europe published troubling reports of objects fireballing across the skies of Sweden and Norway, and even crashing into inland lakes. Considering how much terror and death had rained down from the skies during the war, the sightings of the "ghost rockets" and "spook bombs" seem like phantom afterimages burned into Europe's soul, remnants of the horrors of the fire bombings and the first atomic weapons.

Others speculate that throughout the war there had been fierce rumors that the Germans were nearing completion of a secret weapon that would suddenly turn the tide. By war's end, it was said, the "plate-shaped aeroforms" were either destroyed or, according to conspiracy-minded neo-Nazi groups, spirited away to what is now the secret launching site for flying saucers—Antarctica.

Because intelligence officers had discovered that the Nazis were also experimenting with the first intercontinental missile, designed to carry bombs directly to North America, and because of the rampant fear in Europe that the Soviet Union may have captured some dangerous military technology at war's end, the nearly 1,000 sightings scratching the skies of Sweden and Norway that year had terrifying implications.

At the time, most people imagined them to simply be more rockets, secret Russian weapons developed from the German V-2 rocket program. But

Mystery rocket seen fireballing over Sweden in 1946.

others saw sparking pinwheels or "seagulls without heads," apparently flexible fliers that spit orange and green flames, and could soar, dive, reverse, appear, and disappear at gravity-defying will—sometimes with an eerie whistling sound, sometimes silently.

Even though the Swedish defense ministry went on the record to account for 80 percent of the rocketlike sightings as natural phenomena, about 200 cases couldn't be ascribed to natural deception, foreign aircraft, or common misperception. The commander-in-chief of the investigation also had to admit, in a pattern that would become increasingly familiar around the world, that there was still no proof "that a test of rocket projectiles has taken place," nor should the government dismiss the reports as "pure public imagination." The gap between those two admissions about the "ghost rockets," as they became known, was an open invitation to speculation.

In the late 1940s, there was only a "tantalizing inconclusiveness" to the riddle of the aerial shows that had been loop-the-looping over the skies of Europe and America.

Book Guide

Dragons
Peter Hogarth with Val Clery
(Viking Press, 1980)

The Eye
Francis Huxley
(Thames and Hudson, 1992)

The Great Airship Mystery
Dan Cohen
(Dodd, Mead, 1981)

Mysterious Beings
John Keel
(Doubleday, 1970)

The
Second Wave:

From the Craze to
the Cover-up

*We don't know what it is . . . we don't know
where it's from . . . but we do know it's like nothing we've ever seen before. . . . This may be the
biggest thing that's ever happened.*

—from *It Came from Outer Space*

In *Hamlet*, the tragic hero warns Horatio that there are more things in heaven and earth than dreamed of in his philosophy. Shakespeare's humbling admonition has been borne out during the twentieth century, as the mysterious appearances in the heavens and on earth have repeatedly defied not only our philosophy, but our science, religion, and politics. After the agony and the ecstasy, the horrors and the heroics, from Dresden and Hiroshima to Lindbergh and Earhart, that have transpired in the skies in our century, people have come to expect the unexpected. The surreal has slowly become the norm.

In the summer of 1949, two gold prospectors working in the sweltering heat of Death Valley, California, reported that a peculiar disk-shaped object landed near them. The miners also staked their reputations on the news that two alien creatures who reminded them of dwarfs escaped into the dunes upon being pursued, apparently left behind when the disk vanished.

On May 11, 1950, Paul Trent, a farmer in McMinnville, Oregon, was alarmed when his wife shouted from the yard where she was at her tasks feeding rabbits. A spectacular metallic disk was floating silently over their land. Trent snapped two grainy but distinct black-and-white photographs of the strangely turreted craft before it raced away into the western sky. The Trents didn't develop the film until some time later. When neighbors finally saw the pictures, it wasn't long before the photos reached the local newspaper and were immediately published. The news bolted around the world that the first photographs of a flying saucer had been taken.

For the next forty years the world would scrutinize the dramatic images of a dark object hovering over a simple farmyard the way the Church examines claims of a miracle. Yet they have never been dismissed as fraudulent, even by the critical Condon Committee in 1969.

In March 1950 Navy Commander R. McLaughlin, of the White Sands Missile Range in New Mexico, published an article in *True* magazine describing how scientists tracking a high-altitude Skyhook balloon observed a silvery object that they estimated to be forty feet wide and one hundred feet long, and traveling fifty-six miles overhead at a speed of 25,200 miles per hour. McLaughlin's professional conclusion was that it was "a flying saucer, and further, that these disks are spaceships from another planet."

The next year, over a two-week period between August and September 1951, scores of people witnessed an eccentric light show in the night skies over Lubbock, Texas. Four professors from Texas Technical College watched from a porch as the blue objects glowed like "strings of beads in a crescent shape." The "Lubbock Lights," as they became known, were estimated by the professors to be whipping across the sky at 1,800 miles an hour, and the next day the Air Defense Command radar station clocked the puzzling objects flying at 13,000 feet—at a still stunning 900 miles per hour.

An American colleague of British ufologist John Spencer told him, "All Lubbock ever had was Buddy Holly and the lights, and now they've only got the lights."

In November 1953 Air Force pilot Lieutenant Felix Moncla, Jr., and radar man Lieutenant R. R. Wilson were dispatched in an

"This is one of the few UFO reports in which all factors investigated, geometric, psychological and physical, appear to be consistent with the assertion that an extraordinary flying object, silvery, metallic, disk-shaped, tens of meters in diameter, and evidently artificial, flew within sight of two witnesses. . . . there are some physical factors, such as the accuracy of certain photometric measures of the two original negatives, which argue against fabrication."

—Condon Committee report on the McMinnville photographs

F-89 all-weather interceptor from Kinross Air Force Base, near the Soo Locks in Michigan's Upper Peninsula. Their mission was to track an unidentified object flying at 500 miles per hour over Lake Superior. They were never heard from again. The last twilight zone trace of them was on the radar screen. It showed them approaching 8,000 feet as they passed over the Keweenaw Point. Precisely at that point, their "blip" and that of the UFO converged, then disappeared. One of the attending radar officers later said, "It seems incredible, but the blip apparently just swallowed our F-89."

The official line from the Pentagon was that the UFO was nothing but a Royal Canadian Air Force C-47; but they had no explanation for the disappearance of the American F-89. To this day it is an "unknown." The Canadian government denied the involvement of any of their aircraft.

During the wild UFO wave across the United States in early November 1957, Sheriff Weir Clem and Officer A. J. Fowler of Levelland, Texas, responded to a local farmhand's urgent call that a 200-foot-long elliptical UFO had just flown over his truck, "with a great sound and a rush of wind." Somehow the truck's engine and lights had died. Ten other independent reports within the immediate vicinity corroborated the alarm, seven of which also claimed mechanical failures. In the early morning hours, Sheriff Clem and his deputy discovered the UFO for themselves, "oval-shaped" and glowing "like a brilliant red sunset," just as

Published in 1950 by Major Donald E. Keyhoe, an early and vigorous opponent of the military cover-up of the UFO phenomenon, this classic book sold half a million copies worldwide.

large as reported, passing over Route 116 a few hundred yards ahead.

For three nights in late June 1959, Reverend William B. Gill and as many as thirty-seven members of his Boianai mission in Papua New Guinea watched for up to four hours at a time as a double-decker UFO containing four humanoid figures hovered overhead. The entire object appeared luminous, and the figures seemed to manipulate machinery and even waved to the shocked onlookers below. Four other UFOs joined the "mother ship." On the second night, the Reverend grew bored because "they wouldn't come down, after all the waving." He retired inside the mission for dinner and Evensong services.

For John Spencer the single weirdest encounter took place in September 1955. Poking along the road one day on his moped and presumably daydreaming, one Josef Wanderka somehow drove right up a UFO landing ramp and straight into the arms of tall aliens. Not forgetting his manners, he apologized and must have been doubly stunned when they replied in German that they had just dropped in from the constellation of Cassiopeia. Like any good hosts, they asked him how his little moped operated, and after an anti-Nazi lecture tossed him off the spacecraft, but not without reminding him about the virtues of world peace.

It Came from . . . the Movies!

It was all the crafty world of science fiction could do to keep up with the shenanigans in the skies.

Since the earliest films of Georges Méliès, such as *A Trip to the Moon*, from 1902, the exuberance of UFO witnesses has only been matched by the wild enthusiasm of sci-fi films. The "space operas" are a marvelous mix of Lewis Carroll looking glasses, Jorge Luis Borges labyrinths, Edgar Allan Poe Gothic castles, and Jules Verne intergalactic morality plays. What report or study could ever capture the strange anticipation or "exquisite panic" surrounding the UFO and alien phenomenon as the remarkable phrase *The Creeping Unknown* does? The title of this obscure movie about the sole survivor of a space-flight demonized by an alien microbe somehow conveys the elusive *something* in the dark night of the UFO soul that draws us nearer as it sits there "licking its chops," as H. L. Mencken so eerily put it.

While the UFO debate raged between those demanding "hard evidence" and those vouching for the sacred revelations they truly believed had materialized, a third scenario was already available at the neighborhood cinemas. The sheer accessibility of the movies conveyed for millions what was too often lost in the usually inaccessible debate between believers and skeptics. Just as Marianne Moore defined poetry as being "imaginary gardens with real toads in them," the fantastic atmosphere of the UFO phenomenon during the 1950s took root in our imagination through the very real *images* of movies.

For every UFO study written up and filed away, millions of movie tickets were being sold to people who were more than content to be fascinated by the blood rush of the "riddle" of UFOs, rather than the "answers." At drive-ins, matinees, and midnight shows, sci-fi flicks like *The Thing* and *The Day the Earth Stood Still* captured—and sometimes anticipated—the changing worldview, as influenced by the UFO spectacle. Although the films were often derided, then and now, it was in the darkened theaters that most people got their sensory images of UFOs, and their opportunity to evaluate the meaning of life on other planets, space travel, and invasion of our world.

Besides providing terrific entertainment and often necessary escapism, these films still mirror many of the corrosive concerns of the times: identity, the fear of science, the distrust of technology, and the suspicion, as anthropologist Per Schelde has written, that "science and technology are slowly invading our minds and bodies, making us more mechanical, more like machines."

The roots of the sci-fi craze of the 1950s go all the way back to the nineteenth century, when fantastic fiction that romanticized science and technology was wildly popular. But science fiction took an even firmer grip on the cultural imagination when it was combined with horror films during the fifties. It was then possible to vividly depict an era reeling under the threat of nuclear war, and the fear of dehumanization undermining modern culture. In cautionary and unnerving tales—mirroring the actual UFO and early contact stories—that resist usual interpretation, the world is seen as being overwhelmed by a science gone bad, soulless technology that saves time and money but stills our beating hearts and suspends the awe that deepens one's awareness of life. The banks of flickering computer lights and clever but soulless robots like Robby in *Forbidden Planet*, unnatural machines of sci-fi, symbolize our fear of becoming artificially intelligent. This fear was intensified by what author Ursula K. Le Guin has named "the schizoid arrogance of modern scientism," a science run amok that proclaimed to have answers to many of the ancient mysteries, but in an equally mysterious manner attributed little value or meaning to them.

It Came, It Saw, It Didn't Conquer

One of the most intriguing viewpoints of the time was seen in the 1953 science-fiction thriller *It Came from Outer Space*, in which the gelatinous, floating "eye in the sky" from various world mythologies was mutated into an alien creature's "compound eye." Clever camera work showing the alien's point of view uncannily revealed how our worldview had been recently turned upside down—or was it inside out? Showing our heroes, John and Ellen (Richard Carlson and Barbara Rush), in its fly-eye lens also revealed "us" in the early years of the UFO "invasion," confused, but exhilarated at the implications of *being seen* from above and beyond. The movie became a powerful symbol for a generation's response to the reports from around the world that Earth was being visited—or invaded—in a way that defied conventional explanation.

In the emerging "them or us" scenario of the deeply polarized times, it often appeared that imagery that spoke to the deep imagination wasn't going to be found in hidebound statistical analysis, but at the local Lido. In movies we loved to hate and hated to love, from *The Crawling Eye* and *Attack of the 50 Foot Woman* to *Them!*, *The Thing*, *Invasion of the Body Snatchers*, and *The Day the Earth Stood Still*, there was a cathartic outlet for rampant anxieties about a world gone berserk with atomic testing and biological experiments everybody pretended to admire but nobody trusted.

With America embroiled in another war, and the gulf between science and the public becoming greater, screenwriters hammered out increasingly bizarre scripts in an effort to keep up with the stranger-than-fiction UFO incidents flaring up all over the globe, not to mention the startling advances of more conventional science.

Photo courtesy of Universal Pictures

Universal Studios film *It Came from Outer Space*

At their worst they were paranoid "Red Scare" fables about the imminent invasion of our mind, body, soul, and community; at their best they were gentle reminders about humanity's still undeveloped intellectual and spiritual capacity, and optimistic tales about our evolution.

We may not yet know the truth about UFOs, but we do know that the stories they have seeded reflect certain truths about ourselves and the way our convoluted imaginations work in dealing with the unknown. Our terror of what science and technology have wrought and our anxiety about what the "heavenly powers" or foreign entities might have in store for us are addressed in that powerful mythic image of the alien's compound eye in *It Came from Outer Space*, which told an entire generation that aliens may not mean us any harm after all.

Only a year before, in 1952, Albert Einstein had pleaded with the Pentagon to reconsider its order to shoot down the perplexing UFOs that were buzzing the Capitol building in Washington that summer. This, in turn, had transpired only a year after the vivid portrayal of the trigger-happy military gunning down peace-offering alien Klaatu (played by Michael Rennie) on the Washington mall in a classic "Shoot first and ask questions later" scenario in *The Day the Earth Stood Still*.

Was life imitating art, or art imitating life imitating art? Which of the three episodes, in retrospect, was more preposterous? Or auspicious?

It's helpful to recall that "imagination," as our hero John tells us in *It Came from Outer Space*, "is the willingness to believe that there are things we don't understand," even if it isolates us. Peter Siskind reminds us in his study of movies in the fifties, *Seeing and Believing*, that John is described by the suspicious townspeople as "more than odd. He's individual and lonely. He's a man who thinks for himself." In other words, he embodies the isolation many were beginning to feel about the unsettling UFO phenomenon.

And so this is how we learned "what to think about Martians," as Schelde writes in *Androids, Humanoids, and other Science-Fiction Monsters,* his book on science fiction and the soul—through "movies that present an entire 'worldview,' an 'ideology,' a philosophy about the beginning or the ends of things." The godfathers of science fiction, Jules Verne and H. G. Wells, were influenced by the technology of their time, as reflected in their visions of time travel, space journeys, and alien confrontations. Shows like *Star Trek* have mirrored the common belief in the *strangeness* of the modern quantum view of the universe. What is often at stake in sci-fi is "the interplay between science's most profitable invention, the machine, and the human beings who have to operate [and] program them," as Schelde writes. "Will machines conquer us?" he asks. "Will they eventually dominate us? . . . what's really at stake is the sense of self, or 'soul.'"

While the rampant fear of invasion was still portrayed vividly in allegorical movies like *The War of the Worlds* and in "blob" films such as *Them!,* there was yet another possibility to consider: that aliens from the back of beyond were simply . . . lost in space.

"Don't be afraid. We don't want to hurt you," the creature from *It Came from Outer Space* intones in a stainless steel voice presaging HAL in *2001: A Space Odyssey,* fifteen years before Kubrick's film. "We have souls and minds, and we are good." The alien confesses that they have been hiding because they can't comprehend our need to destroy, a sentiment echoed in thousands of reports from contactees in the years that have followed.

That sentiment didn't come out of thin air. The scriptwriters could have been taking notes at one of the Intergalactic Conventions that were cropping up around the country, as Americans began to think about the possibility of real contact.

Contact!

It was as inevitable as the sunrise. After thousands of reports of strange craft that no government or military in the world would claim and no film crew would admit as a runaway movie prop, someone, somewhere, would say they had been *contacted*.

In 1953 George Adamski, a self-described "philosopher and teacher" who worked as a short-order cook at a café in the shadow of Mount Palomar in California, staked his claim to intergalactic fame with the book *Flying Saucers Have Landed*, in which he tells the world he has become the first human being to meet a visitor from a flying saucer.

Adamski entered American folklore by boasting to anyone who would listen on the lecture circuit how he and four friends driving on the highway from Desert Center, California, to Parker, Arizona, had spotted an enormous cigar-shaped, silvery ship hovering overhead. The craft beckoned the group telepathically to drive onto a dirt road while it followed. Obsessed with proving what he says he had seen many times over the previous several years, he set up his telescope and camera just as a "beautiful craft appeared to be drifting through a saddle between two of the mountain peaks."

A while later, an alien appeared before him, a startlingly handsome creature of average height, suntanned, blond, and long haired, wearing a glossy brown uniform. This wise and loving being communicated with Adamski telepathically and by using sign language. After describing himself as hailing from the planet Venus, the entity said that his craft was powered by magnetism, that he and his people also believed in God, and that some of their craft had crashed on Earth after being gunned down. He would not allow a photograph to be taken because he wished to remain unidentifiable.

Adamski was tapping into a common belief at the time that nearby planets such as Mars and Venus might harbor life. With the flare of the impresario, he gained instant notoriety with his traveling road show of provocative photographs and fantastic tales of his "Space Brothers" that sounded as if they were right out of the pages of the *Amazing Stories!* magazines that sold by the gazillions in those years. His personal accounts of joyriding voyages through the solar system with his other alien contacts—from Mars, Jupiter, and Saturn—also echoed sci-fi films in their platitudinous warnings that there was great alarm throughout the solar system over the development and testing of nuclear weapons on Earth.

Adamski's colorfully bizarre stories helped inspire the first UFO conventions, gatherings of kindred spirits who either wanted to discuss the possibility of science fiction come true, or to share their own revelations of "contact," ranging from benevolent to malevolent. Daniel and Helen Reeve gushed in their 1957 book, *Flying Saucer Pilgrimage*, about a 1954 press conference in Detroit, in which "the questioning and photographing lasted several hours. Mr. Adamski was standing up under the barrage. He was doing more than that; he was gradually creating a miracle, a lessening of skepticism and an increase of respect!" Of a later radio interview with Adamski they write, "An unusual feeling of sincerity was sensed. A thrill stole over the broadcast room. Technicians and helpers paused in their work to listen—almost in awe—to this simple man who told of his contact . . . with a man from another world." At these gatherings there developed the same pattern of lectures warning again of the dangers of nuclear war, the pitfalls of

Outlandish sci-fi artwork flourished in the 1950s, as in this edition of *Flying Saucers Have Landed.*

materialism, and encroaching moral degeneracy, mixed with a certain fondness for "vaguely uplifting sentiments on love." While reminiscent of the turn-of-the-century spiritualist mediums, these sessions were also a preview of the channelers to come.

In 1953 another cosmically inspired contactee, George Van Tassel, founded the College of Universal Wisdom at Giant Rock in the desert near Twentynine Palms, California. Its star attraction was the legendary "Integraton" rejuvenation machine, a kind of cosmic hybrid of a perpetual motion machine and a fountain of youth. In 1954 he organized his first Interplanetary Spacecraft Convention, which attracted 5,000 avid UFO buffs amid wild media coverage. Van Tassel continued to collect funds for the perpetually unfinished invention until he died in 1978.

His epitaph, channeled through a being named Lo, reads: "Birth through Induction . . . Death through Short Circuit." Devotees regularly convene at Giant Rock for its "natural receptivity," as admirers of Adamski still meet at Mount Palomar to share their visions of an intergalactic future.

In his book *UFO Encounters & Beyond*, Jerome Clark places the cults that sometimes arise around "Space Age religious visionaries" into historical perspective. He wrote that in other times and places they would have been interpreters of messages from the gods and goddesses, the spirits or angels.

"*If you threaten to extend your own violence, this Earth of yours will be reduced to a burned-out cinder. Your choice is simple, join us and live in peace or pursue your present course and face obliteration.*"

—from *The Day the Earth Stood Still*

"Can't Miss" Flicks of

The Day the Earth Stood Still (1951)
Director Robert Wise's nuclear age antiwar allegory stars Michael Rennie as a space-traveling Christ figure sent to steer mankind away from its suicidal race toward annihilation. Sam Jaffe is the Albert Einstein stand-in, Patricia Neal the intellectual love interest, and Gort the Robot an outer space enforcer.—R. Beban

The Thing (1951)
The movie poster shouted: "Your blood will turn ice-cold!" In Howard Hawks's classic thriller, American scientists and military personnel stationed in Greenland find a crashed flying saucer. With the help of thermal bombs they free an eight-foot-tall "super carrot" monster from beneath the ice. (Could that be James Arness under all that ice?) When thawed it feeds on human blood and terrorizes the outpost in humanoid form. The movie's closing line haunted a generation: "Watch the skies!"

Invaders from Mars (1953)
In William Cameron Menzie's classic Red Scare allegory, a young boy lives out a nightmare when he wakes up in the middle of the night to witness the arrival of a flying saucer. His parents become possessed by aliens and the race against the clock is on: will young David McLean save them—and the rest of humanity—from being enslaved by the "hordes of green monsters" with sinister plans?

Interplanetary the Fifties

It Came from Outer Space (1953)

An alien spacecraft crash-lands in the Arizona desert. Jellyfishlike aliens occupy human bodies in order to repair their ship for return, and a mystical astronomer intervenes to help them before a panicked posse of townfolk can completely wreck interstellar relations. Jack Arnold directed from a Ray Bradbury short story. Filmed in spectacular 3-D.

The War of the Worlds (1953)

H. G. Wells's classic 1898 novel was adapted by Orson Welles for a radio broadcast that made history when it was mistaken as an authentic report of a Martian invasion, causing instant panic and nationwide mayhem. In the movie, further adapted by George Pal, probing Martians arrive en masse in cylindrical spaceships. Their ravaging death rays instantly vaporize all in sight, transforming the world into a battlefield. In a plot twist, they're defeated not by the befuddled hero, Gene Barry, but by Earth's bacteria!

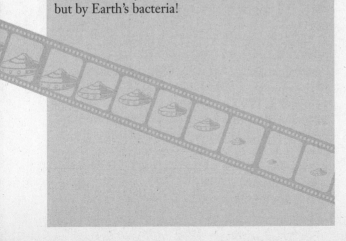

"Can't Miss" Flicks of

This Island Earth (1955)

Scientist Rex Reason solves the ultimate techno-nerd's puzzle-builder, an "interocitor" advertised in a mysterious catalog sent from an unknown source. The intergalactic puzzle leads to a dying race of pompadoured spacemen from the planet Metaluna, and is highlighted by marvelous period special effects including flying saucers, death rays, and a mantislike alien. Sultry Howard Hughes protégée Faith Domergue, a B-movie queen, screams her way through this one, as the companion scientist.—R. B.

Earth vs. the Flying Saucers (1956)

A misunderstood peace message leads to a war between aliens and the armies of Earth. Great special effects from the master, Ray Harryhausen, include saucers crashing into the Capitol and the Washington Monument. Based on the book *The Flying Saucers Are Real,* by Marine major Donald E. Keyhoe, one of the first UFO conspiracy theorists.—R. B.

Forbidden Planet (1956)

Imagine, if you will, a Freudian take on Shakespeare's *Tempest* played out on a distant planet called Altair Four. It's the year 2200, and Earthmen have arrived in their saucer-shaped cruiser to visit a colony that has been on this planet—with a pink desert and a green sky punctuated with two moons—for twenty years. Featuring Robby the Robot (the model for TV's *Lost In Space* robot), who fashions bejeweled clothes and replicates

Interplanetary
the Fifties

bourbon in his belly; Doc Morbius (played by crusty Walter Pidgeon), the sole male survivor of the colony; his daughter, Alta (Anne Francis), who has never kissed a man; and pre–*Naked Gun* Leslie Nielsen as an amorous commander. There's also brainbooster technology developed by an extinct species and a mysteriously murderous unconscious "force" to contend with.

I Married a Monster from Outer Space (1957)
Coming home from his bachelor party, Bill Farrell is engulfed by a hideous space creature who takes over his body. "Bill" (Tom Tryon) marries Marge (Gloria Talbot), who immediately notices his cold, emotionless behavior. Eventually more aliens who have hidden their ships in the woods take over the bodies of many men, in order to propagate and re-populate their planet, Andromeda. A consistently underrated must-see.

—Richard Beban is a reformed film critic and
screenwriter on hiatus.

Calm-down or Cover-up?

While the discussion on the UFO craze may have been lighthearted around the barber's chair or the newspaper office, the subject didn't appear quite so harmless or innocent to the United States military. In the late 1940s there was still considerable concern, verging on obsession, about a possible Communist attack. So whether the sightings were attributed to mass hysteria, a spiritual vacuum, mythic archetypes, or alien spacecraft, because "the saucers were found in the sky and not on the dinner table," the Air Force was assigned the task of getting to the bottom of a problem that was potentially open to exploitation by the Soviet Union. So fraught with anxiety were the times, it was conjectured that the Russians might actually use their own trawlers to release balloons, triggering the release of squadrons of American bombers. To the top brass in Washington, the UFO business was nonsense, but dangerous nonsense that had to be confronted head-on.

By the early 1950s the sightings were as common as, well, flying dragons over medieval Europe! In *Flying Saucers and Common Sense*, Waveney Girvan, an English author and eventual UFO convert, wrote of the typically cool reception the English gave to the phenomenon: "It was, I believe, the sheer weight of these American sightings that led many people [in England] to dismiss the whole thing as a form of mass hysteria to which the Americans are supposed to be prone."

What if these things stirring around above us were Russian reconnaissance aircraft of an unknown type? While Patricia Neal in *The Day the Earth Stood Still* only had to remember to say "Klaatu barada nikto!" to prevent the alien robot Gort from demolishing Washington, the military had run out of charmed words. Instead, they either heaped scorn and satire on those who came forth with their exhilarating sighting stories, or provided pseudoscientific dismissals. These explanations ranged from optical illusions, mental mirages, and temperature inversions, to reflections, refractions, ionized air, lenticular clouds, floating cobwebs, sun dogs, undersuns, and haze layers. But the sightings not only didn't go away, they multiplied like the pods from the movie *Invasion of the Body Snatchers* into what the Air Force began calling "flaps," periods of multiple sightings of entire flotillas of flying saucers.

Military interpretations had already lost a great deal of credibility after the Mantell incident. The ludicrous pronouncement that a highly trained Air Force pilot had died while in pursuit of *the planet Venus* wedged open the gap between believers and skeptics wider than ever. Suspicion percolated that more was known than was being told. The pressure was on the Air Force to solve once and for all the enigma of UFOs, and the implications were disturbing. If the objects were neither Russian nor American, if they were outmaneuvering our pilots with stupefying technology—what were they? Where were they from? Why have they come? How can we calm everybody down?

The V-173 or "Flying Flapjack," a wingless, saucer-shaped experimental plane developed by the navy and flown in more than 100 test flights, but rendered obsolete by orthodox jet fighters. Now on display at the Smithsonian. (Official U.S. Navy photo.)

Photo courtesy of the National Air and Space Museum

The Official Stance

As early as the summer of 1947 the Air Force had secretly begun to analyze the reports of flying saucers by handing them over to the Technical Intelligence Division of Air Material Command at Wright Patterson Air Force Base in Dayton, Ohio. Their official position was that the bizarre sightings were merely honest misperceptions, with a few hoaxes thrown in. But their own postwar jitters (with which they would soon charge the public) had created a fear that Russian secret weapons, built using technology developed by the Germans at the clandestine Peenemünde rocket works during World War II, were infiltrating American airspace. After the war, secret plans had been found at the V-2 works, including elaborate drawings for a saucer-shaped aircraft, and Avro Canada had developed the VZ-9AV saucer shape. A secret weapon shaped like the legendary saucers of the tabloids and sci-fi magazines was no longer fantasy.

Photo courtesy of the National Archives

Ironically, the AV-7055 "flying disk," a highly touted secret military aircraft built by the U.S. Air Force in the early 1950s, was based on recovered blueprints seized from the Peenemünde rocket works in Germany after World War II. Powered by a huge ducted fan, it flew a few feet in the air several times—and then was withdrawn from the military arsenal.

On September 23, the head of Air Material Command, Lieutenant General Nathan F. Twining, concluded that "the phenomenon reported is something real and not visionary or fictitious." For the next nine months Project Sign, the Air Force investigation team, continued its inquiry. Only a few days after the sighting by an Eastern Airlines DC-3 pilot, their "Estimate of the Situation," stamped TOP SECRET, gave a startling endorsement of the "extraterrestrial hypothesis" for the possible origins of the UFOs. General Hoyt S. Vandenberg, chief of staff, rejected the conclusion for lack of proof.

The investigation team and operating procedures were revamped in 1949. The newly renamed Project Grudge team (perhaps an unwitting hint that its primary goal was public relations rather than investigation) came to a conclusion that antagonized everybody involved, essentially that any UFO defying conventional explanation could be explained in psychological terms as abnormal psychology, gullibility, or a hoax.

The official "Project Grudge Report" was a 600-page compilation of 244 UFO cases recorded since the end of World War II in Europe and the United States. In the report, it was admitted that fifty-six cases, or 23 percent, defied easy explanation. Though it didn't dare conjecture what those UFOs might happen to be, it did say intelligent life could conceivably exist on other planets, beings whose technological progress might have begun thousands of years ago. Such an advanced civilization might be here

> *"We, ourselves, look back on an era when many people believed in the existence of centaurs, mermaids, and fire-breathing dragons. I am afraid that twenty-first-century scientists will contemplate with wonder the fact that, in an age of science such as ours, the United States Air Force was required to sponsor repeated studies of UFOs."*
> —Dr. William Markowitz, professor of physics, Marquette University

to scout the planet. The report went on to say: "Its members might observe, that on earth we now have A-bombs and are fast developing rockets. In view of the past history of mankind they should be alarmed. We should expect at this time, above all, to behold such visitations."

Thinking that the furor had subsided, the military was in the process of shutting down Project Grudge when another wave of daytime sightings, many by military and commercial airline pilots, caused them to "upgrade" the team and rename it yet again. Project Blue Book was commanded by Captain Edward J. Ruppelt. His first order was for every U.S. Air Force group in the world to report local sightings.

"In June, 1952," Ruppelt reported, "the Air Force was taking the UFO problem seriously. One of the reasons was that there were a lot of good UFO reports coming in from Korea. Fighter pilots reported seeing silver-colored spheres or discs on several occasions, and radar in Japan, Okinawa, and in Korea had tracked unidentified targets."

That year, a record 1,501 sighting reports were logged. The most spectacular occurred during July over the Capitol building in Washington, an event UFO buffs call the "Washington National Sightings." When seven unidentified blips were detected on radar, the Air Force Air Defense Command scrambled two F-94 jet interceptors after the UFOs. They circled the city without sighting the craft, which suddenly vanished. A week later the blips re-

> "What power urges them at such terrible speeds through the sky? Who, or what, is aboard? Where do they come from? Why are they here? What are the intentions of the beings who control them? Before these awesome questions, science—and mankind—can yet only halt in wonder. Answers may come in a generation—or tomorrow. Somewhere in the dark skies there may be those who know."
>
> —*Life* magazine, April 7, 1952

turned, and after two more F-94s were launched, there came a terrifying moment of indecision when one pilot radioed that the mystery lights had surrounded his jet. He asked whether he should open fire, and while ground control was deliberating the UFOs disappeared.

The Department of Defense held a rather lively press conference the next morning. Major General John Samford launched his own UFO, an unidentified flying opinion, so to speak, dismissed hours later by the government, when he said that UFOs had "unlimited power—that means power of such fantastic higher limits that it is theoretically unlimited—it's not anything we can understand."

Shortly after, the CIA formed the Robertson Panel in January of 1953. For three days they studied seventy-five UFO cases and concluded that although there was no discernible threat to national security, the "continued emphasis on the reporting of these phenomena does result in a threat." Essentially, they recommended debunking the enthusiasts as kooks, the witnesses as cranks. Their only suggestions were for an elaborate disinformation campaign and surveillance for independent UFO research groups that had recently sprung up around the country.

Drawing by Steve Lafler/Courtesy of Regent Press

Artist's sketch depicting the famous sightings of seven UFOs over Washington D.C. in 1952.

Project Blue Book

"They are incredible stories told by credible people."
—Major General John Samford

The letters "U", "C", "S" and "TS" indicate respectively that the information is unclassified or is classified CONFIDENTIAL, SECRET or TOP SECRET.

THE RELEVANT DOCUMENTS

4.   In processing the plaintiff's FOIA request, a total of two hundred and thirty-nine documents were located in NSA files. Seventy-nine of these documents originated with other government agencies and have been referred by NSA to those agencies for their direct response to the plaintiff. One document, which I addressed in paragraph 20c of my public affidavit, was erroneously treated as part of the subject matter of plaintiff's FOIA request. It is an account by a person

Sample page from twenty-one-page top secret affidavit outlining the National Security Agency's position in withholding UFO documentation.

Project Blue Book was the third official study commissioned by the Air Force. At the time, each air base had an officer assigned to report on every UFO sighting in the surrounding area. In turn, their reports were sent on to teams of scientists for technological analysis and certified before being passed to the Pentagon, where the information was then classified. Their standard eight-page questionnaires, photographs, negatives, and film were evaluated, along with occasional on-site interviews, then experts were consulted on applicable data such as meteorological conditions and local flight schedules.

When handling the unsolvable cases, the investigators usually resorted to explanations of natural phenomena rather than admit that the causes for the UFOs were unknown.

The result is an enormous collection of UFO reports that sits in the National Archives, cases in a study that culminated in a remarkable conclusion posed in 1969 when the government slammed the books on the official investigation—that there was nothing warranting further study:

1. That no unidentified flying object has ever posed a threat to national security.

2. That no evidence has been submitted to indicate that unidentified sightings represent technological developments beyond the range of our scientific knowledge.

3. That there is no evidence that the sighted objects are of an extraterrestrial nature.

The Founding of the Center for UFO Studies

"When you get reports from professors at MIT, engineers on balloon projects, military and commercial pilots, and air-traffic controllers, you might one day sit down and say to yourself, 'Just how long am I going to keep calling all these people crazy?'"

—J. Allen Hynek, *OMNI*, 1984

Based on his reputation as a skeptical observer of the rash of saucer sightings, Dr. J. Allen Hynek, professor emeritus and chairman of the Department of Astronomy at Northwestern University, was chosen by the U.S. Air Force as its chief scientific consultant to the infamous Project Blue Book. Yet the appointment backfired on the skeptical government. After studying the vast evidence, Hynek was startled to find the preponderance of reports were from pilots, ship's officers, police officers, and technicians, not just civilians. He became chagrined and disappointed that the scientific world wasn't sufficiently "agog, furiously curious and anxious for answers." By 1973 he had became a "reformed ufologist." That year, inspired by another tumultuous wave of sightings and the "caliber of witnesses" he had encountered for twenty-five years, he

The 1906 and 1987 appearances of Halley's Comet also frame the life of Dr. J. Allen Hynek, astronomer, chief investigator for Project Blue Book, and cofounder of the Center for UFO Studies.

Photo courtesy of Russell Croop

cofounded, with Sherman J. Larsen, the Center for UFO Studies (CUFOS) in Evanston, Illinois, which he directed until his death in 1986.

Other important research groups have included the now-disbanded National Investigations Committee on Aerial Phenomena (NICAP), and the Mutual UFO Network (MUFON).

The Condon Report

After the flap over the flap of the "swamp gas" affair around Ann Arbor, Michigan, in 1966, then-representative Gerald R. Ford was forced to call for an independent scientific investigation of the UFO situation. Officially the study began in October 1966, a startling admission that nearly twenty years of investigations had failed to "get rid of the UFO problem," as Ruppelt said, much less plumb the depths of the mystery.

J. Allen Hynek wrote in the *Saturday Evening Post* after a dinner meeting with members of the newly appointed committee, "What a pleasure it was to sit down with men who were open-minded about UFOs, who did not look at me as though I were a Martian myself." The six scientists who testified before the House Committee on Space and Astronautics on July 29, 1968, agreed that UFOs needed serious investigation. Dr. Hynek remarked that "there is scientific paydirt in a UFO study, possibly very important paydirt, but there may also be scientific quicksand." Fellow committee member Dr. Baker suggested a study that would face the problem of "panic neurosis" that might develop in the event of a "possible encounter with a possible extraterrestrial intelligence." Dr. Carl Sagan

> *"These objects are conceived and directed by intelligent beings of a very high order. They probably do not originate in our solar system, perhaps not even in our galaxy."*
> —Dr. Hermann Oberth, German rocket expert, 1954

admitted that, "It is not beyond any question of doubt that we could be visited," but recommended that radio astronomy and unmanned planetary flights be stressed.

Yet the archskeptic Dr. Edward Condon himself had shown his cards when he said at the outset that his inclination was to tell the government *before the study commenced* that they should "get out of the UFO business" because there was nothing to it. The project's legitimacy was further jeopardized when one of the staff scientists came across a memo by Project Administrator Robert J. Low, which read: "The trick would be, I think, to describe the project so that, to the public, it would appear a totally objective study but, to the scientific community, would present the image of a group of nonbelievers trying their best to be objective but having an almost zero expectation of finding a [flying] saucer."

After investigating only eighty-seven UFO sightings out of the 25,000 reports gathered by Project Blue Book, Condon's summary, published in 1969, asserted that all "careful consideration of the record . . . leads us to conclude that further extensive study of UFOs probably cannot be justified on the expectation that science will be advanced thereby." Yet it created questions galore by listing 25 percent of its analyzed cases as *unsolved*, while stretching all believability with their "natural" explanations of another 8 percent. The cavalier attitude is perhaps better understood in light of Jacques Vallee's later conversation with Condon. As Vallee discussed at the 1992 MUFON Symposium, "He thought a study of UFOs a waste of time not because the problem didn't exist, but because it was outside the realm of science."

Hynek's response to the report was outrage, not only for its misleading nature but because, as Keith Thompson has trenchantly pointed out in *Angels and Aliens*, the report's "most glaring and inexcusable error" was *philosophical*.

In the *Bulletin of Atomic Scientists*, Hynek wrote that, "both the public and the project staff apparently have confused the UFO problem with the ETH (extraterrestrial intelligence hypothesis). This may hold the greatest popular interest, but it is not the issue. The issue is: Does a legitimate UFO phenomenon exist? It may be that the UFO phenomena are . . . inexplicable in twentieth-century physics. From this point of view how does the Condon Report serve science when it suggests that a phenomenon which has been reported by many thousands of people over so long a time is unworthy of further scientific attention?"

The confusion between the two vastly different phenomena was only increasing, and the Condon Report had done nothing to relieve it. It only gave the government the excuse it was looking for to close down Project Blue Book, which it did in 1969.

"Clearly it would be bad public relations for the air force to admit there were things going on in the air over which they claim mastery, which were potentially frightening and over which they could exercise no control. Far better to dismiss the whole thing as public hysteria, hallucinations, IFOs, and even as subversive propaganda than to admit openly that they had a problem that needed study and solution. So, following Pentagon guidelines, Project Blue Book officers did their best to downplay UFO reports that were puzzling and to publicize those UFO reports that could easily be explained and which, therefore, were not UFO reports in the first place. Time and again, I witnessed deliberate attempts to withhold from the media information about 'good' UFO reports, and the distribution of ad hoc explanations for puzzling cases to get the media off their back."

—J. Allen Hynek, *OMNI*, 1984

76

Top Ten Space Tunes

1 **Telestar,** Tornados 1962

2 **Rocket Man,** Elton John 1972

3 **Star Wars,** Meco 1977

4 **Outer Limits,** Marketts 1964

5 **Purple People Eater,** Sheb Wooley 1958

6 **8 Miles High,** Byrds 1966

7 **Martian Hop,** Ran Dells 1963

8 **Fly Me to the Moon,** Joe Harnell 1963

9 **Flying Saucers,** Buchanan & Goodman 1956

10 **The Astronaut,** Bill Dana 1962

—Courtesy of Beatnik Bob

Book Guide

Project Blue Book
edited by Brad Steiger (Ballantine Books, 1976)

The Report on UFOs
Edward Ruppelt (Doubleday, 1955)

The Science Fiction Source Book
edited by David Wingrove
(Van Nostrand Reinhold Company, 1984)

UFO Encounters & Beyond
Jerome Clark (Signet, 1993)

UFOs: 1947 to 1987
edited by Evans & Spencer (Fortean Tomes, 1987)

UFOs: The Public Deceived
Philip Klass (Prometheus, 1983)

IFOs:

Identified Flying Objects and Other Natural Deceptions

The atmosphere is like a deep sea of gases. We are all at the bottom looking up—and strange effects can result from this.

—Jenny Randles,
Director of Investigations, BUFORA

How many of us today can identify the different kinds of clouds and lightning, the curious anomalies of the sky, such as green fireballs or St. Elmo's Fire? How many can distinguish a comet from a satellite, or Venus, Mars, and Jupiter from a distant aircraft?

During our gradual transition from a rural to an urban culture over the last century, we have been steadily losing our ability to understand, experience, and describe nature. As author and naturalist Edward Hoagland has said, "People are losing the capacity to fathom any nature outside of their own." Despite the advancement of science and the slew of nature programs on public television, it apparently hasn't become any easier. When our encounters with the natural world turn from beautiful to baffling and on to what J. Allen Hynek called "high strangeness," then what?

As Allan Hendry, former director of the Center for UFO Studies, wrote in his enormously useful study *The UFO Handbook*, "the great majority of sightings had prosaic explanations; they represented faulty perception of natural and man-made stimuli."

But can it also work the other way around? If a seasoned police officer can mistake Jupiter for a menacing flying saucer, as happened in one of Hendry's cases, or if moviegoers believe flights of wild geese reflected by streetlights to be a squadron of nighttime space cruisers, can natural phenomena also be equally misidentified as the cause behind a genuinely *unidentifiable* aerial object?

When the Air Defense Command scrambled those infamous F-94s in June 1952 to pursue the seven baffling UFOs that were mocking the radar screens around Washington D.C., they were chasing phantoms that eluded not only their best planes but also easy definition.

Speaking of the UFOs that returned to haunt the U.S. Capitol on July 20, Captain C. Pierman, a commercial pilot, said, "In my seventeen years of flying I've seen a lot of falling or shooting stars, but these

81

lights were much faster than anything like that. They were about the same size as the brighter stars, and much higher than my 6,000 feet. Please remember I don't speak of them as flying saucers, only very fast moving lights."

Imagine the chaos in southeastern Michigan on March 19–20, 1966. Frank Mannor and his boy watched incredulously as a fiery football-shaped object as big as a car lingered over the swampland near their farmhouse for half an hour. At once, they notified the local Dexter–Ann Arbor police, who were startled to watch the UFO fly over their own patrol car as they drove to the Mannor house to investigate. The next night eighty-seven coeds saw the UFO hovering for four hours over the swamp near their campus. When the official Project Blue Book investigator, J. Allen Hynek, arrived and was pressured to quickly solve the riddle (remember what fate the Sphinx had in store for those who couldn't answer her riddle!), he improvised a seemingly logical source for the mystery lights. The hastily convened press conference echoed the official explanations of the first wave of sightings in the late 1940s: "mild cases of meteorological jitters." To account for the crackling noises and glimmering lights reported over the previous few weeks, Hynek conjured up a phrase that would haunt him the rest of his life: swamp gas.

Archskeptic Donald H. Menzel was convinced, however, that "studies made by the U.S. Weather Bureau . . . established beyond doubt that the targets were spurious, produced by partial trapping. Radar waves were simply being reflected by bubbles of warm air in the atmosphere."

> "*Air Force, Navy, and commercial pilots have revealed to me when a UFO would fly right off their plane's wing. . . . highly secret government UFO investigations are going on that we don't know about.*"
> —Senator Barry Goldwater

Patrolman Lonnie Zamora won't talk anymore about what he saw the night of April 24, 1964, when he was chasing down a speeding car near his hometown of Socorro, New Mexico. After confronting Hynek and the Project Blue Book team of investigators with their most incomprehensible case, he has gone silent on the subject of the strange blue-orange flames and angelic figures that he saw and the deafening roar that forced him off the main highway and through the dark hills.

That night he expected to find an exploded dynamite shack. Instead Zamora encountered an enormous blinding object the size of a car that had landed about 800 feet away from where he stopped. Two small beings stood near the elliptical object until he got out of his car to get a closer look at the shining craft, which rested on four legs and featured an odd insignia on its side. Suddenly the figures disappeared inside the object, which launched off with another deafening roar, followed by a "sharp-toned whine." Before it disappeared into the night, there "was complete silence about the object," as he later recalled. When state trooper M. S. Chavez arrived at the site, he found Zamora in shock.

The actor and comedian Jackie Gleason named his Peekskill, New York, residence "The Mothership" and designed it to resemble a flying saucer.

Together they inspected the area, which revealed what appeared to be the burn marks of a landing site and, nearby, the "footprints" of something humanoid.

The case is considered one of the strongest in the annals of ufology because of Zamora's rock-steady reputation and the physical evidence at the site. Hynek declared, "Of all the Close Encounters of the Third Kind, this is the one that most clearly suggests a 'nuts-and-bolts' physical craft." Adding to the mystery, the civilian investigator, Ray Stanford, reported a craft that matched Zamora's description flying over the same grounds in the days that followed.

And yet the case is equally notorious for debunker Philip Klass's imaginative if not reductionistic explanation of the strange sight as "plasma," ionized gas that sometimes forms into balls of lightning and, according to some theorists, leaps to and fro in the atmosphere.

Swamp gas? Air bubbles? Plasma? "Strange tricks?" as the *Saturday Evening Post* described the way Mother Nature can fool the eye as the atmosphere makes the sun and stars appear to jump around.

How many of those thousands of annual reports are mistaken perceptions of commonsense skylights such as planets, stars, or meteors? Is there another explanation for the seeming wizardry of some aerial phenomena? Or was Margaret Sachs right when she commented that the belief in piloted craft from outer space arises only because of "the twentieth century's space-age interpretations of poorly understood phenomena and the human need to believe in a higher power."?

What did the ancients call the strange lights they encountered? What recent theories best explain the UFO light shows? What is known? What has been identified? Can we learn to tell the difference between a genuine mystery and a hoax? Or between our lack of knowledge about natural phenomena and things that truly defy reductionistic thinking and unimaginative explanations?

The "Ignorasphere"

In the mid-1950s, Scottish physicist and Nobel Prize winner Charles T. R. Wilson observed that the enormous electrical discharges from thunderstorms should have a fascinating effect on the upper atmosphere.

For years, high-altitude pilots have reported seeing bizarre flashes and ghostly lights as they flew above storms, but until 1989 no one had documented them. That year, John Winckler, a professor of physics and astronomy at the University of Minnesota, began to capture on videotape the first images of the eerie bursts and blasts of "blue jets" and "red sprites," as atmospheric scientists are now calling them, high in the strange skies above thunderstorms. In contrast to ordinary lightning bolts or other celestial displays, these flashes are three-dimensional structures that appear in a painter's palette of colors, from orange to salmon, and are shaped like columns, spikes, and blobs, carrots, cauliflower, and octopuses. The blue jets fire out of the crown of thunderstorms at more than 100,000 miles per hour, and the red sprites can reach sixty miles into the dark sky.

Walter Lyons, an atmospheric scientist at Mission Research Corporation in Fort Collins, Colorado, under contract from NASA, set up a video camera on nearby Yucca Ridge in the summer of 1993 for an unobstructed view of the lightning-and-thunder-riddled Great Plains. Among the nearly 1,000 optical flashes that he and his coworkers have captured on camera since then is an "Angel of Death" fluttering her wings in the stratosphere high above a violent thunderstorm. "She" appeared like a long white-robed figure, then vanished—halo of dancing light and all—after a few hundredths of a second. Lyons adds, "We've got one called the Bird, one called the Blessed Trinity. And then we've got the Dancing Carrots."

At the 1994 American Geophysical Union Conference in San Francisco, scientists discussed these thrilling celestial events now considered to be tremendous surges of energy between the layer of atmosphere known as the mesophere, and the thermosphere, which is well above the stratosphere at the very edge of space. "That part of the sky has also been called the 'ignorasphere,' for good reason," said Davis Sentman of the University of Alaska's Geophysical Institute. "We were ignorant of it."

Superbolts of lightning? Clouds of electric fields that ionize the air until it glows like fluorescent lightbulbs?

For Winckler, the phenomenon of strange light flashes in the night sky still defies explanation. "We're in on the beginning of a new aspect of science here." Meanwhile, groups of skywatchers gather nightly in Colorado, Kansas, and Nebraska to record the dozens of sprites streaking from thunderstorms in the heavens.

"All we know for now," says Lyons, "is that the more we look above thunderstorms, the weirder it gets."

Natural Deceptions

If the sky continues to defy experts and civilians alike, the confusion over the strange aerial displays becomes more understandable.

According to John Spencer, in *The UFO Encyclopedia*, the number of UFO cases eventually solved is between 90 and 95 percent, with the majority of natural deceptions coming from astronomical sources, such as particularly bright stars and planets, followed by aircraft lights, meteor showers, and satellites.

Most of the reported UFO sightings, as determined by Allan Hendry, are eventually explained as misperceptions of unusual astronomical or aeronautical phenomena, and a range of other anomalous lights and shapes in the sky. After personally analyzing more than 1,300 reports that came in on his UFO hot line at CUFOS in 1976–77, Hendry concluded that 8.6 percent eluded his eventual identification and remained tantalizingly unknown.

As we've seen, it's hard enough to keep up with the mysteries of the shape-shifting heavens. Is it possible to learn how to identify what Hendry calls the "UFO impostors"? Though he frames the issue by stating that "the likelihood of hoax, fantasy, or misperception has always clouded the issue of positively determining UFO status," he adds that anyone can

Distortions

Stylized flowchart illustrating how natural phenomena and man-made aircraft can be easily mistaken for UFOs when observed through the atmospheric filters of fog, haze, reflections, mist, and ice crystals.

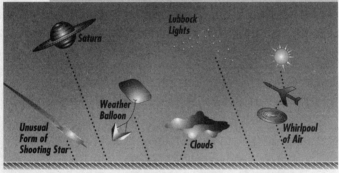

FOG — HAZE — REFLECTIONS — MIST — ICE CRYSTALS

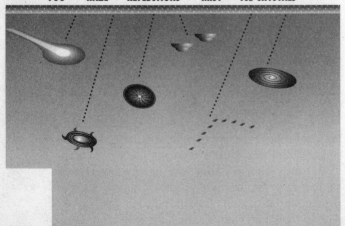

identify a good "90 percent of UFO reports" with a modest amount of information about what can be misinterpreted.

The "ordinary explanations," as British researcher Jenny Randles terms them, range from clouds of electrified air, optical illusions, mirages, or meteors, what are called IFOs (identified flying objects), in contrast to their notorious unidentified cousins.

When all is said and done, analyzed, and cross-referenced, a small but significant portion of UFO sightings, from 3 to 10 percent, depending on your source, elude conventional explanation. Considering the thousands of reports logged around the world since the late 1940s, that leaves a considerable number of unexplained cases. The statistics can never diminish the power these sightings or encounters have had over the witnesses. If anything, it is humbling to realize again and again how nature seems to shapeshift from age to age, as our understanding of her wily ways rises and falls, disappears or deepens.

But then there are the cases that demand even more, such as the phosphorescent UFO that startled the poor fishermen near a forest in the English Midlands. After some brilliant deduction worthy of Sherlock Holmes, it was determined that the UFO was an *airborne owl* literally glowing in the dark after a late-night snack of decaying fungi!

Skylights

Luminous displays have long haunted the sky and taunted the earth. Flaming spheres, spinning fire disks, glowing, whirling wheels, electric effulgence, phosphorescent gleams, and celestial medusae: a litany of colorful phrases has been used when reporting UFOs through the centuries.

Some skyborne phenomena include unusual clouds, the most breathtaking being the mellifluously named lenticular, or lens-shaped, clouds, which, when floating through a deep blue sky, could easily be mistaken for majestic airships.

Then there are sun dogs, also called mock suns or parhelia. These are peculiar solar reflections through ice crystals in the atmosphere. They are optical illusions of a second sun and are often reported by pilots or airline passengers as "flying disks."

Photo courtesy of Jerome Wyckoff

Sun dogs, also known as mock suns or parhelia, are often reported as UFOs. They occur when the sun's rays are reflected off of ice particles in the air, generally at sunset.

Photo courtesy of Dick Ruhl

Lenticular, or lens-shaped, clouds are often mistaken for UFOs. This aerial armada was seen floating over Brazil in the mid-1950s.

Other NLs (nocturnal lights) that bedevil people include refracted starlight, shifting night clouds that create the illusion of bright objects appearing and disappearing, and the sometimes mesmerizing glow of planets, usually on the horizon. Jupiter, Mars, and Saturn have all been reported as UFOs at one time or another, but Venus tends to be the most popular in UFO folklore.

Allan Hendry reports how during World War II, the USS *Houston* fired 250 rounds of ammunition at Venus, while the gunnery officer kept bellowing, "Lengthen your range, lengthen your range!" Another amusing anecdote comes from the FAA official at Detroit Metropolitan Airport who asked: "Do you know how many times we've cleared Venus to land?"

Mechanical IFOs

As the skies have grown more crowded in the twentieth century, it isn't surprising that a considerable number of UFO reports turn out to be modern aircraft. Those most frequently mistaken for otherworldly craft include common airplanes, large research balloons and weather balloons, kites, blimps, zeppelins, advertising planes with "light strings," and jettisoned spacecraft junk.

Several classic examples of UFOs attributed to everyday occurrences come from debunker Donald H. Menzel. He dismissed the famed Lubbock Lights in Texas with a harrumphing analysis claiming that either streetlights, car headlights, or house lights were reflecting off a layer of haze just above the heads of the witnesses. Menzel's verdict on the Washington flyby UFOs of 1952 was "temperature inversion," despite the original air-traffic controller's livid response that professionals are plenty familiar with the anomalous weather conditions that turn up on their radar screens.

In the early 1970s bright white lights appeared almost nightly in the skies over the Yakima Indian Reservation in south-central Washington state. They were observed most often by Indian lookouts atop their fire observation towers, but other reports filtered in from witnesses claiming encounters and even abductions. W. J. Vogel, in the May/June 1984 issue of *International UFO Reporter*, recounts the story of a couple driving east on U.S. 220 at 4 A.M. when a light the size of a basketball and as high as a tall building floodlit an area about a mile in diameter, interfered with their car radio, and dimmed their headlights. The light suddenly went out, and something "sped up into the sky at an extremely high rate of speed and disappeared."

Earth Magic

The ancients believed in earth magic. Intuitively or through shamanic visions, they sensed that certain places were sacred or conducive to contemplation, ritual, rite, and regeneration. Investigations by the British researcher Francis Hitching, among others, have suggested that many of these "sacred sites" on which megalithic stones were placed in antiquity, as were cathedrals in later eras, are centers of terrestrial magnetism and high electromagnetic activity, often with underground streams running below. In the nineteenth century British researchers trying to determine a pattern behind the apparent order of the approximately 200,000 megalithic sites concluded that they could be connected with straight lines. Their "ley line" theory is similar to what the Chinese

In 1966 Gerald Ford cited widespread dissatisfaction with the official response to the Ann Arbor "swamp gas" sightings and concluded: "In the firm belief that the American public deserves a better explanation than that thus far given by the Air Force, I strongly recommend that there be a committee investigation [of the UFO phenomenon]."

geomancers call "dragon paths," hypothetical lines of earth force between sites of heightened earth powers.

The dragon path theory may or may not turn out to be mere superstition. It is humbling to recall that until recently meteorologists rejected the reality of the rare but natural atmospheric condition of ball lightning, glowing spheres of ionized air. While traditionally reported in the valleys of Norway and off ships at sea, the condition has become associated more recently as the reputed source of many UFO reports.

Earthlights:
The Tectonic Stress Theory

Since the early 1980s investigations by Paul Devereux in the United Kingdom and Michael Persinger in Ontario, Canada, have pursued what appears to be a modern counterpart of the earth magic idea. As fire-snorting dragons have long been associated with the old stone sites of Europe—perhaps a mythic image of the coiled energy believed to dwell there—bewildering reports of earthlights have recently become associated with UFOs.

By suggesting that natural causes are behind the UFO phenomenon, the earthlight theory attempts to connect the strain of the movement of the planet's tectonic plates and other geophysical activity with the "sparks" of luminous lights linked with UFO sightings. Although not vouching that tectonic strain is the "motor for UFO appearances," Devereux does believe we have the "first glimmerings" of the long-sought-after mechanism that triggers the dazzling lights that appear to witnesses as alien spacecraft.

Going beyond aviation writer and debunker Philip J. Klass's "plasma" hypothesis, expounded in *UFOs Identified*, Michael Persinger and Dr. Brian Brady's TST (Tectonic Stress Theory) offers an explanation for an increase in UFO reports weeks or

Soft Objects

In contrast to "hard object" UFO sightings, "soft object" UFOs are bright light displays, usually nocturnal, that are reported to have an uncanny "intelligence" behind them as they transform into craftlike clouds, fireballs, or phantom lights.

months before earthquakes. Brady's experiments at the U.S. Geological Survey laboratory have shown that stress in certain rocks can produce hot ionized gases seen as balls of light. The implication is that intense tectonic activity produces correspondingly large luminous balls of energy or fire, along with bursts of radio frequency. According to the theory, electrical charges create lights that tend to move erratically around the landscape, creating the illusion of zigzagging, death-defying spacecraft.

Occasionally plasma scenarios have been developed by scientists to explain previously perplexing UFO cases. In August 1979 Minnesota police officer Val Johnson reported an enormous, terrifying bright light zooming down the highway straight at him, forcing him off the road and colliding with his car. Proponents have pounced on the case as an example of an outbreak of earthlights. Persinger tries to account for such visions as the result of electromagnetic phenomena rising from earth strain that causes the brain to create a phantasmagoria of visions, including spacecraft landing lights and abduction scenarios. In other words, brain strain feigns aliens.

Opponents resent the reductionism and lack of proof. Chris Rutkowski, chairman of Project UFO Canada, has asked why we don't hear about UFO reports with each earth tremor. Rutkowski concludes that, while it is engaging, the theory that underground electromagnetic energy creates luminous balls that are large enough and last above ground long enough to fool people into believing they're UFOs "involves such tenuous assumptions that it cannot be accepted without a great many misgivings."

Crop Circles

"Electromagnetohydrodynamical Vortices" is what Britain's foremost expert, Professor Terence Meaden, calls them. Also known as crop circles, cornfield circles, agriglyphs, unusual ground mark-

Worldwide Crop Circle Organizations

CCCS (Centre for Crop Circle Studies)
P.O. Box 146, Guildford, Surrey GU2 SJY
United Kingdom
Publications: *The Circular; The Journal for Crop Circle
Studies*

CERES (Circles Effect Research Society)
3 Selborne Court, Tavistock Close
Romsey, Hants S051 7TY, United Kingdom
Publication: *The Crop Watcher*

**CNACCS (Center for North American
Crop Circle Studies)**
P.O. Box 4766, Lutherville, MD 21094

**NAICCR (North American Institute for
Crop Circle Research)**
649 Silverstone Avenue
Winnipeg, Manitoba R3T 2V8, Canada

**TORRO (Tornado and Storm
Research Organization)**
54 Frome Road, Bradford-on-Avon
Wiltshire BA15 ILD, United Kingdom
Publication: *Journal of Meteorology*

ings, saucer nests, and UFO landing nests, they are, according to John Spencer, "circular flattened areas of wheat and other crop fields which periodically occur during the spring and summer in many areas of southern England . . . and also in Europe, Australia and America." These extremely popular sites are most memorable for their symmetrical patterns, sometimes occurring as simple flattened circles, but also appearing in a wide variety of layouts that resemble Indian petroglyphs, mathematical formulas, and Vulcan tattoos.

Crop circles are one of the most confounding and astounding earth mysteries and a first cousin to the UFO sky mystery. Many "cereologists," or crop circle experts, say they are undoubtedly linked to UFOs. One connection is that some crop circles have been discovered in locations where UFO sighting activity has been heavy. One spectacular single clockwise swirl was formed in a field of long grass in Gulf Breeze, Florida, in 1989, close to the location of Ed Walters's controversial reports of UFO encounters.

Many who believe we are being visited by extraterrestrials have claimed that crop circles are simply "UFO nests" or "launch pads," and at first look they do resemble some of the physical evidence connected to UFOs. Most serious ufologists have suspended their judgment of this saucer nest theory, however, because the differences between the two phenomena suggest there's too much of a disparity:

Crop Circles
- invariably occur in crops
- neatly avoid field boundaries
- never harm the crops or earth
- make ornate shapes, swirls, and patterns

UFO Landings
- can gouge into rocky or hard earth
- can make depressions in various terrain
- can scorch or burn vegetation
- can make simple circles or linear marks

Although close to a hundred UGMs (unusual ground markings) have been recorded every year in North America since 1990, according to NAICCR (North American Institute for Crop Circle Research), it is believed that thousands have appeared in Great Britain, and, in lesser numbers, in other parts of Europe and Australia since they came to wide public attention in the late 1980s.

The meaning of the symbols, as well as their origin, has been the subject of much study and debate. Eyewitnesses have reported "strong spiraling downdraughts" making these "cookie cutter" patches in the grasses, leading some to explain the phenomenon as an "atmospheric vortex," or just strong electric winds. Some say this luminous energy can explain thousands of UFOs seen spinning close to the ground or even higher in the sky.

Another hypothesis is the TIF (Theory of the Intelligent Force), which suggests these agriglyphs were propelled into being by "ultraterrestrials" or other intelligent life. Just as UFOs come in many shapes and sizes, the crop formations come in an array of patterns, with any number of satellite or "grapeshot" markings that can appear gradually over varying periods of time. The ornate pictograms, including rings around circles, keys, arrows, wheels within "donuts," and countless others, often attract curiosity-seekers from miles around.

Book Guide

The Crop Circle Enigma
edited by Ralph Noyes
(Gateway Books, 1990)

Earth Magic
Francis Hitching
(Picador, 1976)

The UFO Encyclopedia
compiled and edited by John Spencer
(Avon Books, 1991)

UFOs & How to See Them
Jenny Randles
(Sterling Publishing Co., 1992)

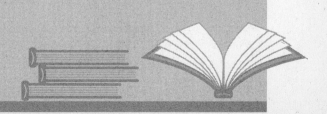

The Third Wave:

Encounters, Intruders, and Abductions

Before the cylinder fell there was a general per-suasion that through all the deep of space no life existed beyond the petty surface of our own minute sphere. . . . We know now that in the early years of the twentieth century this world was being watched closely by intelligences greater than man's across an immense ethereal gulf, minds that are to our minds as our minds are to the beasts in the jungle. Intellects, vast, cool, and unsympathetic, regarded this earth with envious eyes, and surely drew their plans against us.

—H. G. Wells, *The War of the Worlds*

The suspicion that we are being watched from above by intelligences greater than ours and visited by a strange range of "uninvited guests" has taken on a wild life of its own since the end of World War II. Detailed reports of extraordinary alien encounters including kidnappings on dark country roads, midnight visitations shrouded in blue light, and genetic experiments performed on the cold steel-like operating tables of time-warping spacecraft have touched the deepest recesses of the modern imagination. As we approach the millennium they are likely to increase.

Together, the reports express an almost hypnotic mix of science, mysticism, and front-page urgency. So much so that, "It is easy to find ourselves entranced," as psychologist Kenneth Ring writes in *The Omega Project*, "with a sense of their beguiling, tantalizing mystery as we are caused to wonder what unknown forces may generate such strange experiences into human consciousness."

What do we make of this "invasion" of our imagination, if not our homes or bodies? How do we come to grips with these unknown forces from the back of beyond that dare to disturb our universe? What do we infer from Whitley Strieber's striking observation, "Flights of angels arrive and we call them demons"? How do we resolve the fierce rivalries vying for *the* explanation, theories ranging from the "nuts-and-bolts" hypotheses to "psychological projection," from the twilight world of the tabloids to the stringent analysis of academicians?

Ring writes, "There is in many of us perhaps even a desire not so much to solve the mystery as to savor

> *"We all know that UFOs are real. All we need to ask is where do they come from."*
>
> —Captain Edgar D. Mitchell, Apollo 14 astronaut, after his moonflight in 1971

it, for the appeal of a mystery is precisely that it calls forth our own imaginative and creative potentials." Or as the trickster mythologist Joseph Campbell was fond of saying, "Life isn't a problem to be solved, but a mystery to be experienced."

In their book *Phenomena*, John Michell and Robert R. J. Rickard have navigated between the treacherous rocks of the "hard reality" of scientific rationalism and the "soft reality" of psychological interpretation. In contrast to the polarizing either-or debate, their recognition of "phenomenal reality" has great implications for any consideration of the UFO enigma, because they emphasize the power and validity of what someone has actually experienced, not conceptualized, however unfathomable or absurd that experience might be to the outside investigator.

In the often surreal world of UFOs, the "phenomenal reality" is the report, the story, the tale brought back from an encounter with mystery lights, flying disks, or the mesmerizing stare of an alien being. UFO investigator J. Allen Hynek concluded something similar in his book *The Search for Extraterrestrial Intelligence*, when he said, "I don't talk about UFOs very much anymore. I talk about the UFO *phenomenon*. . . . The phenomenon is the continual flow of reports, now from 140 countries."

The provocation of these stories launches what-if questions about the nature of the universe the way NASA launches rockets: What if we aren't alone in the universe? Why would ETs bother to leap whole galaxies to visit *us*? What would change if it were all true?

"Secrets in the Saucers"

For most people, abduction images come from B-movies, science fiction, and cartoons. These images have evolved considerably since the 1950s, when the oversize tales of notorious hucksters and hoaxers made it difficult for serious ufologists to gain respect. In the last several years even the subject of alien kidnappings has gone mainstream as people have sought out counselors and therapy groups—and television talk show hosts have sought them out to satisfy viewers.

On June 29, 1987, the abduction phenomenon made the pages of the venerable *Washington Post* with a curious tug-and-pull headline: "Secrets in the Saucers: Unidentified Facts Fly at AU Symposium." Their story covered the Mutual UFO Network (MUFON) Eighteenth Annual International Symposium on Unidentified Aerial Phenomena at the American University. Presumably, the "secret" was that a few hearty souls came forth at the convention to reveal what had been transpiring "inside" those legendary saucers these past forty years.

"It was the first abduction that we know of," Shirley A. Coyne told the crowd of 450 ufolks. "I was taken from my bed by two little beings who were two and a half, three feet tall. They came into my bedroom, took me through the living room. . . . It was like we were floating, not walking. I had no control. They took me aboard this craft and gave me an examination. . . . very painful. They did all kinds of little experiments on me. They took a sample from my leg. I have a scar on my thigh where they took a sample of tissue. They did something to my back and other things I'd rather not talk about."

Coyne, a Michigan housewife with two children and three grandchildren, was able to describe her ordeal because she had undergone the controversial practice of regressive hypnosis. While in a trance, she "remembered" a metallic, walnut-shaped craft with whirling, flashing lights, and the lurking presence of "grays," small gray-white beings with "very, very large" eyes. Through hypnosis she came to believe that her abductions began when she was a child of nine and continued into her late teens. Like many others, after the dramatic revelations gained through regression sessions and repeated UFO sightings she has become active in the ufology field.

The UFO Phenomenon
Becomes Personalized

To paraphrase the old movie poster, she is not alone. According to a recent analysis of the 1991 Roper Organization poll on "Unusual Personal Experiences," one in fifty Americans, approximately five million people, are "probably" abductees. Common sense and a healthy dose of skepticism warns us about such figures. If true, and then calibrated for the rest of the world, as science writer Dennis Stacy has done, hundreds of millions of people would "probably" have been abducted now by squadrons of spacecraft stacked up over the world's major cities like 747s circling airports. It's an enormous leap of faith from the poll's fascinating findings about "unusual experiences" to "probable" correlations with alien abduction. A belief in ghosts and UFOs, and experiences of "actually" flying through the air and sensing the presence of strange beings at night are interesting parallels but not equivalents. Nevertheless, the results are important in how they reflect a truly remarkable increase in paranormal beliefs and experiences. What was once considered "supernatural" is apparently becoming mainstream.

Whatever the truth of the numbers involved, there is an exhilaration at the possibility of contact with extraterrestrials. Most people now literally entertain the idea, as reflected not only in the irrepress-

> *"I've often wondered, what if all of us in the world discovered that we were threatened by an outer power from outer space from another planet wouldn't we all of a sudden find that we didn't have any differences between us at all?"*
> —President Ronald Reagan

ible popularity of the tabloids but in our culture's passionate embrace of science-fiction books, fantasy magazines, and video games starring the latest mutation in alien monsters. One new trend is the proliferation over the past decade of abduction-based books and films, such as Whitley Strieber's *Communion*, Budd Hopkins's *Intruders*, and Travis Walton's story, *Fire in the Sky*, which all insist on a real, not merely symbolic, alien presence. It's as if the UFO movement, previously mired in hardware and graphs, has finally been personalized.

The Baffling Roots of the Abduction Movement

While the interest in UFO abductions may be peaking as we approach the millennium, the movement didn't develop overnight. John Godwin vividly describes the often giddy atmosphere of the early 1950s when men and women became instant celebrities based on their colorful claims of being kidnapped, seduced, or taken for joyrides by saucer crews from Mars, Venus, and Jupiter. One man produced drawings of his long-haired Venusian captors wearing Eisenhower jackets and ski pants. Like the Bishop of Ussher pinpointing the exact year of the Creation at 4004 B.C. (at 9 A.M.), a British writer estimated that the first Venusian expedition to Earth arrived in the year 18,617,841 B.C. In southern California, a Los Angeles real estate agent described her Martian visitors as angels of "almost unimaginable beauty."

Truly Extraordinary Encounters

Late in the evening of October 14, 1957, a young Brazilian farmer named Antonio Villas-Boas was tilling his field when he saw a "luminous egg-shaped craft flying toward [him] at terrific speed." When he raced after it the uncanny object evaded him and flew away.

The next night the object reappeared as Villas-Boas rode his tractor. This time it landed directly in front of him, its dome rotating and changing from red to green, and short-circuited his tractor engine. Frightened, he tried to escape, but was dragged on board the UFO by three small humanoids wearing tight gray suits, helmets, and goggles.

Inside the craft, Villas-Boas was stripped, covered with a peculiar liquid, then forced to undergo a medical examination. The next thing he knew he was alone with a female alien who was, he later sighed, the most beautiful woman he had ever seen. He was initiated into intergalactic intimacies, which he described later as "normal," except for her habit of barking like a dog, which, he deduced, was the way the aliens communicated.

After being released, he was alarmed to discover strange wounds all over his body. A local doctor, Olivio Fontes, detected radiation poisoning, a common symptom among people who have claimed contact with alien craft. The simple farmer, who had no previous interest in UFOs, apparently didn't desire to capitalize on his experience. He kept the mystifying episode to himself for eight years, until, in 1965, he answered a notice for UFO stories. He maintained the truth of his claim to the end of his life.

Drawing by Steve Lafler/Courtesy of Regent Press

In the lavender fields of southern France, at dawn on July 1, 1965, farmer Maurice Masse was walking out to his field, a bowl of warm French coffee and a croissant presumably still rumbling in his stomach, when he chanced upon what he believed to be two young boys collecting lavender next to a strange-looking "helicopter." As he drew closer, the farmer was shocked to find that the "boys" turned out to be four-foot-tall alien creatures with domed heads and slit eyes dressed in green uniforms. The copter next to them was a white egg-shaped craft the size of an automobile, perched on six legs, reminding Masse of a spider. Incredulous, the farmer edged closer, only to be "paralyzed" by a ray shot out of a long tube on a belt worn by one of the aliens. By the time Masse had come to his senses, the aliens had reboarded their craft and ascended with a wild high-pitched sound.

For the next ten years, the farmer reported, lavender would not grow in the landing area of the unidentified craft.

This UFO story comes from Jacques Vallee's catalog of more than 900 cases logged from 1868 to 1968. It is but one example from the annals of ufology that are studded with stories that bear repeating for their colorful details and sense of open-ended mystery. The Center for UFO Studies has over 100,000 cases in its database.

"UFO abductees, once largely considered the province of cranks and comic books, have become a mystery that touches on, among other things, sex, psychology, religion, and the presumptions of the Western mind."
—Mark Gauvreau Judge, *Common Boundary*, 1993

Hynek's Parable of the Elk

An elk is wandering through the Northwest Territory when suddenly he sees a strange craft and some very strange creatures. He experiences missing time and eventually wakes up knowing something has happened. The machine and the creatures are gone, but he goes back and tells his fellow elks, all members of B.P.O.E. 347, about his experience. They say, "What kind of moose milk have you been drinking?" Well, he doesn't know it, but the strange craft was actually a helicopter, and the strange creatures, people. They fired a tranquilizing bullet into him, and while he was unconscious, implanted a transponder. So the elk, after he wakes up, has no notion whatever that whenever a certain satellite passes overhead it activates the transponder, and back in Washington D.C. his blood, heartbeat, temperature, and location are all being carefully plotted . . .

—*OMNI*, 1984

The Fantastic Journey

The first abduction story to gain extensive publicity in the United States was that of Betty and Barney Hill's Close Encounter of the Fourth Kind. While driving home through the White Mountains of New Hampshire on the evening of September 19, 1961, the Hills were shocked to see an enormous pancake-shaped object with two rows of windows descending from the sky near Indian Head. Through a pair of binoculars, they observed the erratic motions of the object, which seemed to resemble an airplane fuselage, only it was wingless. At first, they assumed the object was a star or a satellite.

"We were driving along on a tarred road," Betty says in the transcripts of her later hypnosis, "and all of a sudden, without any warning or rhyme or reason or anything, Barney stopped suddenly and made this sharp turn off the highway." Her husband pulled off to the side of the road for a closer look and leaped out of the car. He crept within about fifty feet of what appeared to be an enormous craft with projected fins and whirling red lights. Peering through a row of windows, he was stunned to see six otherworldly beings inside. From the car Betty heard her husband screaming, "I don't believe it. I don't believe it! This is ridiculous!"

Terrified, he dashed back to the car and sped away. Farther down the road, their car began vibrating. They heard an unusual beeping sound, and a haze seemed to fall over them.

> *"Abductions may not represent literal contacts with aliens, but whatever they are, they constitute a strange phenomenon worthy of study from a number of perspectives and by diverse disciplines. . . . Whatever their physical nature, even if they prove to be nothing more than stars and airplanes, their cultural impact has been enormous."*
>
> —Thomas Bullard, *International UFO Reporter,* 1989

109

When they arrived home something felt off-kilter. They checked their watches, which had stopped, and when they calculated their return drive it seemed to have taken much longer than it should have. Inexplicably, they had "lost" two hours some-where along the road.

After the incident, Barney's ulcer began acting up. Then he and Betty began suffering intensely disturb-ing dreams. They were compelled to seek help a few months later from Dr. Benjamin Simon, a Boston psychiatrist. Four months of regressive hypnosis un-raveled the hidden dimensions to their already har-rowing story. By recovering their "missing time," the Hills, independent of each other, recalled under trance how they witnessed the landing of the flying saucer, their subsequent abduction by robotlike be-ings, and humiliating medical examinations con-ducted by the alien crew. They described these aliens as being about five feet tall, hairless, with grayish skin, pear-shaped heads, domed foreheads, and slant-ing catlike eyes. Betty recalled being pierced in her navel for a "pregnancy" test, and being given a "Star Map" so the strange entities could reveal to them they were from a place called Zeta Reticuli.

While their story captivated America, the cultural watchdogs howled. One investigator claimed that the UFO was nothing more than the planet Jupiter. Re-gardless, in 1967 an account of their otherworldly encounter became a best-selling book by John Fuller, aptly titled *The Interrupted Journey*, and in 1975 a

docudrama detailing their story, *The UFO Incident*, was filmed. The case continues to be discussed heatedly in UFO circles.

Undoubtedly, the Hills saw *something*, something strange enough to shatter their ideas about reality—and challenge those of an entire nation. With their vision, the modern era of the UFO abduction phenomenon had begun. Ordinary people who had undergone severe trauma now saw a model of explanation. Many became convinced they too were being kidnapped and floated through the heavens *against their will*.

The Pascagoula Incident

At dusk on October 12, 1973, Charles Hickson and Calvin Parker, two shipyard workers, were fishing from the end of a pier at the Shaupeter shipyard in Pascagoula, Mississippi. Suddenly they had the skin-tingling feeling that something was lurking behind them. They turned and saw an oval structure topped with a strobing blue light. There was a low hissing sound. A hatchway yawned open and three ghostly figures with slits for eyes and pale, wrinkled skin floated toward them.

"They didn't have clothes," Hickson reported. "But they had feet shaped . . . it was more or less a round like thing on a leg, if you'd call it a leg. . . . I was scared to death. And me with the spinning reel out there—it's all I had. I couldn't, well, I was so scared, well, you can't imagine. Calvin done went hysterical on me."

Two aliens seized Hickson with their crablike pincers and the third reached for Parker, who fainted with terror. Hickson felt himself glide into the UFO where he became paralyzed, though still conscious. His recall is understandably hazy about what transpired in the UFO, which he described as around eight feet tall and oblong, with a mechanical "roving eye" inside that gave him the proverbial once-over twice.

Hickson confided to John Spencer in 1987, "I was offered all kinds of money to let them do a movie. I declined. I am still declining. Making money is not what the experience is all about."

After his investigation, Dr. J. Allen Hynek released a press statement: "There's simply no question in my mind that these men have had a very real, frightening experience . . . under no circumstances should these men be ridiculed. They are absolutely honest. They have had a fantastic experience."

Fire in the Arizona Sky

In contrast to the Hickson encounter, the Travis Walton story has become one of the most well known abduction tales of our time, owing to a successful mass-market book and a "major motion picture." On November 5, 1975, the twenty-two-year-old man was heading home with six other members of a forest-clearing team after a day of woodcutting in the Apache-Sitgreaves National Forest near his home in Snowflake, Arizona. Suddenly a "large gold-domed UFO" with windows appeared at treetop height. The driver of their pickup truck, Mark Rogers, stopped long enough for the mesmerized Walton to leap out and dash toward the object. The rest of the crew yelled in vain and then watched in horror as a blue ray from the UFO—the last thing Walton himself saw—lifted him a foot into the air, then thumped him to the ground. So shaken was Rogers, he panicked and roared away, taking the others with him. Ten minutes down the road, cooled down and confident that the UFO had headed back to wherever it had come from, they returned but found no evidence of their friend.

Five days later a scared and shivering Walton, ten to twenty pounds lighter, unshaven, and

> "No significant body of thought has come about that presents strong evidence of anything else happening other than what the abductees have stated."
> —David M. Jacobs

dazed, called his future brother-in-law from a phone booth in Heber, Arizona, several miles away. His story came back to him over the next few days with the help of hypnotic regression. Able to recall just two hours of the entire period, his only memories were of attempted medical examinations performed by fetuslike entities with "large, domed bald heads, huge black eyes, and reduced facial features," and of waking up on the highway miles away just in time to see the UFO catapult into the dark night sky.

The Walton case magnetized UFO buffs and debunkers alike. Twenty years after the blue bolt from the sky, all seven men who were in the truck that night hold firmly to their story.

The Contours of the Abduction Story

Abductions are to UFOs what miracles are to faith, vital to the perpetuation of the mystery of the movement, but unsettling to the more conservative believers. For some, the harrowing tales are proof positive of the menacing reality of extraterrestrial visitation; for others, the outlandish implications are just the evidence they need to put the kibosh on the entire subject. From the accounts of the actual "ex-

Drawing by Steve Lafler/Courtesy of Regent Press

periencers," as abductees sometimes prefer to be called, and the sympathetic experts who are trying to fathom the depths of their stories, it becomes evident that the range of the phenomenon is far wider than even science fiction had dared to roam. We know there are mystifying encounters in the UFO annals, but is there a common pattern, a typical encounter that can be gleaned from the thousands of reports? Could it be helpful for readers who are troubled by their own unexplainable experiences to see their story in the context of a typical encounter?

The Typical Abduction Scenario

Each abduction encounter that has been reported is profoundly personal. After thirty years of reports, a compelling pattern approximating a typical abduction encounter is now being discussed in UFO circles.

The experiencer is driving alone at night and sees something unidentifiable, a light or the shadow of a strange object, moving erratically. They inexplicably pull off the road to watch it.

After being "floated" or carried away by a cosmic light, or seized by "aliens," the abductee becomes enshrouded in a trancelike silence in a round vaulted room filled with light and cold air. A businesslike medical examination on a cold table is performed by alien beings, often under watchful mechanical eyes or scanning devices, or the peculiar and disturbing *staring* of the beings themselves. Biological samples such as hair, skin, sperm or ova, and genetic tissue are taken. Through telepathic communication, messages are conveyed to the

"Whether the abduction is recalled as a dream, or through hypnosis or spontaneously, the nature of the episode is identical. . . . *though UFO investigators often use hypnotic techniques to elicit and explore close encounters . . . these procedures cannot be said to* create *these encounters in the first place."*
　　　—Kenneth Ring,
　　　　The Omega Project

Types of

Forensic expert William L. McDonald created the following alien classification system, based on abductee case reports.

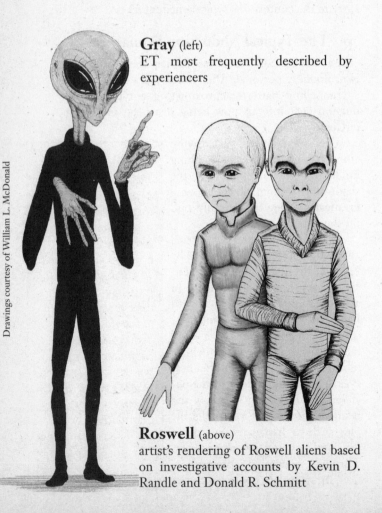

Drawings courtesy of William L. McDonald

Gray (left)
ET most frequently described by experiencers

Roswell (above)
artist's rendering of Roswell aliens based on investigative accounts by Kevin D. Randle and Donald R. Schmitt

Extraterrestrials

Neonate
most fetuslike

Nordic
most humanlike

Reptile
reptilian, with scales and claws; perceived as evil

Hybrid (above)
most childlike, with wispy white hair; said to be
part human

experiencer, ranging from dramatic warnings of the imminent dangers of nuclear war or environmental devastation to reminders of the need for brother-hood and universal love.

The next thing the witness sees is the UFO flying off, in a movielike dissolve, or their own car starting up, or they just seem to "wake up." Startled, relieved, and confused, he or she continues on, but soon real-izes that time has flown by in a twilight zone kind of way, what researcher Budd Hopkins has called the telltale Missing Time Experience (MTE).

Back home, experiencers begin to have bizarre dreams, detect the return of an old illness, find a scar or mark on their body, feel an inner tug-of-war about confiding the encounter to someone else. It is esti-mated that about one-third of abductees sponta-neously recall their encounters, while the rest learn about theirs through the aid of hypnosis.

However the memories are dredged up, one con-stant seems to be that contactees are profoundly changed by their mysterious encounters. The pattern of influence can vary drastically, from bitter paranoia to a newly kindled interest in the welfare of the planet, to a renewed and intensified love of humanity.

To folklorist Thomas Bullard, what is most im-portant about the remarkable patterns in these ab-ductions is not the shared concepts determined later, but that all abductees have a "shared experience."

Peering Inside the UFOs

"Something's wrong, something's not quite right," as the Doors sang in the late 1960s. Missing time, paralysis, scars, food offerings, post-traumatic stress, space-and-time-defying journeys? Do the common traits of the abduction phenomenon sound unprece-dented? Do they feel peculiar to our time? Are we "abdicating responsibility" if we ignore all the troubling signs, as Budd Hopkins told Michael Lindemann in their published conversation in 1990?

For David M. Jacobs, history professor at Temple University in Philadelphia, what is most intriguing about the abduction encounters is their uniqueness; this is a phenomenon unprecedented in form as well as in its implication for the future of humanity. And most intriguing for UFO buffs, Jacobs believes that the encounters are the missing link in understanding the entire enigma: *why* the aliens are here.

"Taking a close look at the abduction phenomenon gave us our first insight into the motivations of the intelligence behind UFOs," he said in his address to the MUFON Symposium in 1987. "It was as if a door had opened and we were able to look inside the phenomenon . . . of extraterrestrial life, motivations, intentions, and activities. . . . We may be on the threshold of momentous discoveries."

After Jacobs's classic study *The UFO Controversy in America* was published in 1975, he began an investigation into more than 300 abduction cases. He rejected the notion of mere psychological fantasies because he was intrigued by the accumulation of minute detail, including the impersonal nature of the contacts, the evidence of unusual physical scars, and the cases of multiple abductions. Feeling as if he were peering into a hidden world, Jacobs named his second book *Secret Life*. In it, he emerged with a three-tiered model for the range of the abduction phenomenon:

1. Primary experiences: physical examinations, staring, and urological and gynecological experiments.

2. Secondary experiences: examination by machine, visualization, and a child-presentation procedure.

3. Ancillary experiences: physical, mental, or telepathic displays, and sexual activities.

At the core of his findings is his belief in a program of manipulation of human beings by a technology and superior intelligence for the conception, gestation, or incubation of hybrid babies. He says that "one of the purposes for which UFOs travel to Earth is to abduct humans to help aliens produce other Beings. It is not a program of reproduction, but one of *production*. They are not here to help us. They have their own agenda, and we are not allowed to know its full parameters."

For Jacobs, the abduction scenario isn't "benign in any way, shape, or form," as he told *Common Boundary* magazine in 1993. Instead, he warned, all we see of the visitors "is a dispassionate clinical program fulfilling an agenda of their own that has very little to do with us except to use our bodies for their own purposes."

Jacobs, along with other abduction experts, is so convinced of the literalness and seriousness of the abductee problem that he has little patience for the psychosocial, cultural, government conspiracy, and collective unconscious viewpoints of the phenomena. His work edges past academic commentary into an old prophet's warning of an alien invasion that is already under way, one we don't take seriously at our own peril.

The Spiritual Dimension of Abduction

In his best-selling book *Abduction*, John Mack covers the gamut in response to the phenomenon. One of his clients, Anne, is quoted as saying ominously, in a tone that recalls our ancestors talking about the gods or the fates, "Something else is interested in us that we don't want to know about. . . . This is really a responsibility, and things that you don't want to see happen are going to happen."

For Mack, a highly regarded psychologist and Pulitzer Prize-winning author, "The only theory that makes any sense is that what's happening is exactly what the people say is happening to them. Namely, that some kind of entity, some intelligence, is coming into our world, taking people, and doing things."

In contrast to the interpretations of David Jacobs and Budd Hopkins, Mack estimates that what the "aliens" are doing is not all bad. Instead, "with the opening of consciousness to new domains of being, abductees encounter patterns and a design of life that brings them a profound sense of interconnectedness in the universe." Mack recounts how one patient, Dave, in his response to an abduction, began to see synchronicities, or "meaningful coincidences," all around him. Another man, Arthur, interpreted the shining thread that carried him to a UFO when he was a boy as the tie that bound his life to others. A middle-aged health-care executive described passing through large tubes during an abduction "into the next plane where there was this light. . . . It was like a birth because there was fluid in the tubes."

Mack has explored the same territory as Jacobs and Hopkins but emerged with a different map. The abduction scenario is not evil, as others have projected, but benevolent, "at its core, about the preservation of life on Earth at a time when the planet's life is profoundly threatened." For many abductees, Mack has noticed, their encounters have triggered in them a renewed interest in the deep causes of the times, from ecological awareness to spiritual crisis to the need to stave off nuclear war. He has gleaned

"I could not believe the intensity of what I was feeling. I was sobbing like I haven't since I was a kid, sobbing, sobbing, almost hysterical. Even if I could dismiss everything else as being a fantasy or some kind of delusion or some kind of confabulation, I can't dismiss how intensely I felt, the absolute terror. You have an experience like that, and it shatters your base of reality."
—Catherine, a twenty-five-year-old abductee

from his own interviews that the "oceanic" feeling of interconnectedness reported from so many of his patients is the tie that will bind, the force that will move us beyond ourselves, and it "appears to be love."

The Visitor Experience

On the night after Christmas, 1985, Whitley Strieber, the author of such mindbending horror novels as *The Wolfen* and *The Hunger*, experienced something as bizarre as anything out of his own books, what he came to call "a genuine enigma."

Under regressive hypnosis, Strieber pieced together the fragments of an abduction memory, apparently only the latest in a series that dated back to his childhood. He was startled awake by "a peculiar whooshing, swirling noise coming from the living room downstairs," then realized that an alien creature with "two dark holes for eyes and a black downturning line of a mouth that later became an O" was approaching his bed. The rest of the night is a terrified blur, only fugitive images of being paralyzed in a dark wood, entities in dark-blue coveralls performing a bizarre operation on his head with "an extremely shiny, hair-thin needle mounted on a black surface," and more gruesome procedures. Finally, he awoke at dawn, disturbed by the sense of a nightlong struggle and a provocative memory "of seeing a barn owl staring at me through the window sometime during the night."

My stars! Where in the world?

From channelers and experiencers to scriptwriters, everyone has a different idea where ETs are from:

Alpha Centauri, Andromeda, Arcturus, Draco, Lyra, Orion, Pleiades, Sirius, and Zeta Reticuli, to name a few...

As recounted in his best-selling book *Communion*, the encounters were "visitations," as if he had, by dint of will, made the aliens his allies and turned what might have been only horrific into an opportunity for spiritual transformation (indeed, his follow-up book is titled *Transformation*).

Strieber's interpretation of what happened to him and others who have endured an abduction episode is rooted in what the mystics term a "soul crisis," a period of deep loss, a struggle with meaninglessness, an inability to feel or move or be moved.

In 1991, in his last *Communion* newsletter (oriented to abductees), Strieber discussed how the abduction phenomenon might reflect the separation of the human soul from nature more than a theme of science fiction. He wrote that the significance of the wave of UFO sightings in the last four decades is a signal that, under the shadow of nuclear threat, the world is steadily going blind to the deep reality of the soul and the ancient and immense realities that the soul has always evoked.

"When a person who yearns inwardly for change reaches the psychological breaking point," Strieber wrote, "the visitors may come in through the cracks in that person's wall of belief. There are things at large in the night of the soul; the visitors live there . . . [they are] the reflection of my own soul."

The Encounter-Prone

Kenneth Ring has discovered a pattern in those who are most likely to report abduction episodes. He calls these people "encounter-prone personalities." Years of work with patients who have undergone near-death experiences (NDEs) have shown him that they possess an "emotional authenticity and are personally compelling of transcendental experiences." After comparing people who had NDEs with UFO abductees, Ring detected in both groups a high incidence of child abuse. For him, the key to the phenomena is how the personality learns to split off.

Ring observed that the most likely candidates to report abduction experiences and other strange encounters are those who have endured trauma. "People with this kind of background," he states, "are more likely to learn as a child to disassociate. Therefore when they experience trauma in later life . . . they're more likely to go into a dissociative state, which in turn would make them more susceptible to what I call alternative realities."

In the phenomenal realm, the way in which we see the world determines the way we live. Imagination is the way of reckoning with the crisis of meaning when we have lost sight of the shore.

For Ring, those who are reporting extraordinary encounters are "extraordinary experiencers, the true visionaries of our time, the bearers of the emerging myth of the twenty-first century calling us to a cosmic-centered view of our place in creation." These often troubled souls may be revealing a new vision of how to see our role in the cosmos, may even have the power "to ignite the fires of a worldwide planetary regeneration and thus to save us from the icy blasts of Thanatos's nuclear winter."

"Although no one can prove that people are actually taken aboard UFOs, if you should find yourself in this predicament, try to remain calm. Observe and remember as much as you can; even ask questions. Try to grab something and bring it back with you as evidence of your experience. As in life, having faith, courage, a sense of humor, and using your intelligence will help you deal with the most unusual situation."

—Brian A. Boras, *UFOs: Q & A's*

If there isn't any one truth, one sweeping explanation, one top secret revelation, what is there? How else can we edge closer to the center of the story without losing the mystery? Are there similar stories, remarkable parallels to the UFO and alien phenomena that can give us deeper insight into both our time and past times? Would it help some troubled souls to consider some uncanny parallels? Would it change anything if we suddenly discovered the "final proof"?

These extraordinary encounters alternately anger, humble, and mystify us. Our assumptions about the boundaries of reality are being confounded with each new report of journeys into the outer reaches of inner space.

Contactee

IF (Intruders Foundation)
P.O. Box 30233
New York, NY 10011
212/645–5278
Publication: *IF Bulletin*
Founded by author and abduction researcher Budd Hopkins to provide support for abductees.

IFUFOCS
(Institute for UFO Contactee Studies)
1425 Steele Street
Laramie, WY 82070
307/745–7897
Publication: Proceedings, transcripts from annual conference.
Conducts the annual Rocky Mountain Conference on UFO Investigations, which features guest speakers and conducts open forums for contactee case discussion and evaluation. Founded by Dr. R. Leo Sprinkle in 1980.

MUFON (Mutual UFO Network, Inc.)
103 Oldtowne Road
Seguin, TX 78155-4099
512/379–9216
John Carpenter, National Director of Abduction Research

Resources

TREAT (Center for Treatment and Research of Experienced Anomalous Trauma)
P.O. Box 728
Ardsley, NY 10502-0728
914/693–8827
Publication: *Paradox* (quarterly)
Provides information and runs conferences for health-care professionals and practitioners on topics related to anomalous trauma, including UFO abductions.

**UFOCCI
(UFO Contact Center International)**
3001 South 288th Street, Suite 304
Federal Way, WA 98003
206/946–2248
Publication: *The Missing Link* (bimonthly)
Dedicated to helping people who have had experiences in connection with UFO sightings. They conduct an annual conference over Labor Day weekend.

Book Guide

Breakthrough
Whitley Strieber (HarperCollins, 1995)

Communion
Whitley Strieber (Century Hutchinson, 1987)

Intruders—The Incredible Visitations at Coply Wood
Budd Hopkins (Random House, 1987)

Missing Time
Budd Hopkins (Richard Merrick, 1981)

The Omega Project: Near-Death Experiences, UFO Encounters, and Mind At Large
Kenneth Ring
(William Morrow and Company, 1992)

Passport to Magonia
Jacques Vallee (Contemporary Books, 1993)

Book Guide

Secret Life
David M. Jacobs, Ph.D. (Simon & Schuster, 1992)

UFO Contact at Pascagoula
Charles Hickson and William Mendez
(write to: 2024 Carol Drive, Gautier, MS 39553)

**Unusual Personal Experiences:
An Analysis of the Data from
Three National Surveys**
conducted by the Roper Organization (1992)

**Visions, Apparitions, Alien Visitors:
A Comparative Study of the
Entity Enigma**
Hilary Evans (The Aquarian Press, 1984)

The Walton Experience
Travis Walton (Berkley Books, 1978)

Uncanny Parallels

Over and over again, this shape-shifter has been telling us: Look for resemblances, larger patterns which connect smaller ones.
—Keith Thompson, *Angels and Aliens*

130

It is said that the Laplanders believed that the aurora borealis is created by spirits holding flaming torches as they escort the souls of the dead across the vault of the heavens and to the afterworld.

In the highlands of Celebes, at the crossroads of the Seven Seas, the Toraja claimed their original ancestors descended by starships from the Pleiades and populated their lush green world.

The *anagaquo* is considered a magical sight to the Eskimo. This inner searchlight spreads throughout the shaman's body then into his head, burning in his brain like a luminous fire that allows him to see in the dark, to perceive things and coming events that are hidden from others.

In World War II, the planes of pilots who were killed in action during the Battle of Britain *carried on the fight* because, as Air Marshal Lord Dowding believed, angels took over the flight controls.

It is known now that science-fiction writer Philip K. Dick suffered from visions of "violent phosphene activity," and in a series of white heat note-writing to his friend Ira Einhorn, some 500,000 words in all, he described how it "did not seem bound by either time or space . . . within my head it communicated with me in the form of a computerlike or AI system—a voice quite different from any human voice, not male or female, and a very beautiful sound it was, the most beautiful sound I ever heard."

Several centuries ago, Saigyo, the Japanese master and poet, wrote:

> Since I no longer think
> of reality
> as reality,
> What reason would I have
> to think of dreams as dreams?

> "For too long the UFO question has been one of polarities. UFOs are spaceships or UFOs do not exist at all."
>
> —Thomas Bullard

The Shape-Shifting Lessons

It appears that weird lights in the sky, bizarre stories of ancestors gliding down from the heavens, odd people gifted with the second sight or unusual powers, violent inner visions and haunting voices, doubts about the thin line between reality and dream, and tales of genies, trolls, elves, and wee people have been repeated in all cultures throughout history.

To paraphrase the philosopher George Santayana, those who don't understand history are condemned to repeat the mistake of thinking their generation has the most inscrutable mysteries of all time. For there are many periods of history in which people lived in an enchanted world where visions were common to a degree that modern people would find difficult to comprehend. In those times, the world was alive. People literally saw things and saw *into* things. Voices were heard, and hearkened. Omens were everywhere. Heralds announced the changing of the guard and the gods.

Is history merely repeating itself with the phantom appearances of UFOs? Or is this anomaly "the greatest scientific adventure of all time," as one UFO historian believes?

The Fairy Tale Parallels

Most European UFO researchers reject the American "extraterrestrial hypothesis" in favor of the "psychosocial hypothesis." Like them, French-born author Jacques Vallee, who now lives and works in the United States, doesn't automatically equate UFOs with extraterrestrial spacecraft, nor does he believe that reports of encounters with strange beings mean we have alien visitors. Instead Vallee ventures into the worlds of folklore and anthropology. Most re-

> *"Stories of diminutive creatures like faeries whisking away unsuspecting humans are common in folklore around the world."*
> —Jacques Vallee

cently, he's confronted the spate of well-devised hoaxes and media misrepresentation—which combine to divert research from exploring the deeper issues of the UFO phenomenon—by asking the daring questions: Are the UFOs "windows" rather than "objects"? Could unusual inner states somehow be responsible for the uncanny UFO encounters?

Vallee's studies in the late 1960s were a daring synthesis of the physical and psychological evidence of alien contact. In his own phrase, it was a "forbidden science" during a time when studying UFO landings was considered fringe even by ufologists, who feared that any sensational findings might prejudice their case before Congress and the Condon Committee.

By exploring ancient and modern records alike, he found a robust worldwide pattern of reported visitations from other worlds that were bewildering and consistent. It was "a continuum of experience and belief where fairies merge into spirits, spirits into the dead, the dead into ghosts, ghosts into apparitions into fairies into extraterrestrials," as folklorist Peter Rojcewicz has so marvelously put it.

Unlike the anthropologists and comparative folklorists who preceded him, Vallee seeks to show how our age is generating "mythical material all unparalleled in quantity and quality," documentation of a re-

An unwilling abductee is dragged away from a shimmering fairy circle, as portrayed in an 1800s engraving by W. Sykes.

current myth, namely the myth of contact between mankind and an intelligent race endowed with apparently supernatural powers.

In his influential book *Passport to Magonia*, Vallee speculates about the nature of UFOs by probing history and discovering fundamental parallels between the "aerial visitors" in the fairy tales and legends of our ancestors and the modern wave of sightings of otherworldly visitors. In his research he has uncovered remarkable correspondences between religious visions, fairy tales, the Great Airship Mystery, and modern UFO sightings, a pattern of parallels in the stories of extraterrestrial visitors who come to earth and perform wonders, influence the course of civilization through revelation, and seduce earthlings. For Vallee, "the modern, global belief in flying saucers and their occupants is identical to an earlier belief in the fairy-faith. The entities described as the pilots of the craft are indistinguishable from the elves, sylphs, and *lutins* of the Middle Ages."

> *"The first of [the fairies] I saw I remember very clearly. . . . there was first a dazzle of light, and then I saw that this came from the heart of a tall figure with a body apparently shaped out of half-transparent or opalescent air, and throughout the body ran a radiant electrical fire, to which the heart seemed the centre. Around the head of this being and through its waving luminous hair, which was blown all about the body like living strands of gold, there appeared flaming wing-like auras. From the being itself light seemed to stream outwards in every direction; and the effect left on me after the vision was one of extraordinary lightness, joyousness or ecstasy."*
>
> —George William Russell (A. E.), Irish poet

Who Are These Fairies?

"Who or what are these fairies that are found in the traditions of all cultures, who bless and manipulate humans, and who poets and writers of romance use for their own purposes? . . . 'the fairies' are supernatural or spiritual beings who, although they possess human emotions and drives, make love and war, live either solitarily or in social groups much like humans do, nevertheless possess power and knowledge greater than ours. Neither gods nor angels, 'the fairies' continually involve themselves in human affairs, utilizing their superiority both to our benefit and detriment. Fairies are generally believed to be shape-shifters, beings capable of manipulating their form at will. Neither of flesh nor pure spirit, fairies are intermediary beings 'betwixt man and angel,' as the Reverend Kirk would have it. . . . Fairies can appear and disappear at will, a trait that parallels the protean nature of 'UFOs.'"

—Professor Peter M. Rojcewicz, folklorist

To illustrate his idea of the parallels, Vallee refers to Walter Wentz's turn-of-the-century studies on the Aran Islands, located off the west coast of Ireland, where "the rocks were full of them." "Old Patsy" told Wentz a "true story about the fairies":

> One day I was gathering berries along a hedge not far from here and something made me turn over a flat stone which I saw in the ditch where I stood. And there beneath the stone was the most beautiful little creature I have ever seen in my life, and he in a hole as smug as could be. He wasn't much larger than a doll and he was most perfectly formed with a little mouth and eyes. I turned the stone over again and ran as hard as I could to bring my mother, but when we got back we couldn't see a thing of him.

Vallee then turns to the rich repository of "landing reports" recorded during the fall of 1954 in France. In this sighting in Pournoy-la-Chetive, Moselle, four children who were roller-skating at dusk suddenly saw a luminous object near the cemetery:

> It was a round machine, about 2.5 meters in diameter, which was standing on three legs. Soon a man came out. He was holding a lighted flashlight in his hand and it blinded us. But we could see that he had large eyes, a face covered with hair and that he was very small, about four feet tall. He was dressed in a sort of black sack like the cassock M. le Curé wears. He looked at us and said something we did not understand. He turned off the flashlight. We became afraid and ran away. When we looked back we saw something in the sky: it was very high, very bright and flew fast.

After decades of research, Vallee has come to believe that the "colorful rumors" of UFOs that have baffled "scientists, theologians, and literary scholars" have behind them an innate mechanism that influences consciousness everywhere. This inner mechanism produces visions, bliss, rapture, and appearances by gods and goddesses, magicians and fairies, flying saucers and aliens, and helps to form consciousness and culture, but is determined by the current system.

Discovering the parallels and blurred borders between the past and present and future worlds puts us "in a very privileged position," as Vallee writes, enabling us to witness a "folklore-in-the-making." The source of these mysteries is so close it's as if "we can almost reach out into the night and grab those lurking entities. We are hot on their trail; the air is still vibrating with excitement, the smell of sulfur is still there when the story is recorded."

Something strange lurks in that twilight world where the stories are unfolding in their own defiant way. Vallee recounts the story of the Air Force colonel who was driving alone one night on a remote Illinois road. Suddenly he noticed a peculiar object flying above his car. It was the size of a small airplane—only it looked like a bird, and *flapped its wings*, then flew away.

Parallel Universes

If that "cosmic chameleon" the UFO has taught us anything, it's that it changes its appearance too often to be explained by any one theory. There are simply too many reports with wildly diverging details and too few patterns to rely on one "theory of everything." Too often the debate disintegrates into an either/or solution. Either UFOs are spaceships from distant and exotic galaxies or they are psychological projections, real or symbolic, benevolent or malevolent. The search for parallels may

> *"My queries reflect my enduring intuition that the UFO is a key of sorts to the human future."*
> —Keith Thompson

help us resolve the debate in ways that stretch our imagination more than our patience.

In her book *Aliens Among Us*, the famous channeler Ruth Montgomery cites a talk delivered by J. Allen Hynek in Brasilia, Brazil, in 1979, in which the globe-trotting ufologist revealed how he had come to see the UFO prodigy as paradoxically both physical and psychological. To bridge the two worlds, Hynek found a unique correspondence between the "low strangeness," so to speak, of behavior at the subatomic level, and the "high strangeness" behavior he attributed to UFO encounters. Hynek noted how "theoretical physicists view light as reacting like particles or waves." Montgomery writes that he then presented a challenge: "If the physicist can accept the dilemma of light-as-particles and light-as-waves, then cannot the UFO investigator equally accept the dilemma of UFOs-as-objects and UFOs-as-psychic events?"

It is into this profoundly chaotic and unpredictable world that UFOs are landing, a world of constant flux, where bizarre things occur at every level of reality and paradox seems to hold sway. From the quantum perspective it is easier to imagine how a

> *"There is a vast array of thousands of guides whose purpose it is to help us human beings on the planet who are in great danger of self-destruction from nuclear weapons. They are here to help us change the tide, to work against the negativity that now threatens our survival. Then there are the personal guides, who are there for each one of us to open to them, to direct us to be more positive. For every person who becomes more positive, the chances of the planet's self-destruction are minimized."*
>
> —Elizabeth Kübler-Ross

strange craft can appear one moment and disappear the next, or to account for the sudden appearance and disappearance of alien visitors, or their alleged ability to move through solid matter. The century's discoveries in quantum physics offer a novel way of dealing with the choplogic tales that fill the pages of UFO encyclopedias. If we begin to consider the quantum possibility, then the question of the "reality" of UFOs becomes a mystery of their behavior: How do they come and go like subatomic particles? Where do they come from? Where do they go when they leave? Under "normal" circumstances we might even wonder how they got here and how long it took. But as Einstein himself wrote in a letter describing his stoic attitude toward the death of his oldest friend only four days before his own death, "the distinction between past, present and future is only a stubbornly persistent illusion."

In his book *Parallel Universes*, physicist Fred Alan Wolf writes about the upheavals in our thinking about the universe since the discoveries of the new physics. Not only is the distinction between different realms of time proving to be an illusion, according to Wolf the past, present, and future may even exist "side by side." Just as *we* are not alone, our universe itself might be accompanied by parallel universes.

> *"As far as the laws of mathematics refer to reality, they are not certain; and so far as they are certain, they do not refer to reality."*
>
> —Albert Einstein

Wolf says, "I believe that visionaries are those who are able to turn away from everyday life concerns and tune in to these other worlds, whether they are past-life recalls from parallel worlds gone-by or future life-recalls from worlds yet-to-be." Those who learn to pick up the signals from the past and the future, he suggests, are those who find a way to live beyond time. The signals might be carried by lucid dreams, premonitions, various mental disorders, or even flying saucer sightings. From the quantum physics point of view, all of these phenomenal realities might be manifestations of other worlds parallel to ours, examples of how "information flows in both directions simultaneously" on the river of time.

"We live in the in-between world . . ." physicist John Barrow has remarked, "betwixt the 'devil' of the quantum world and the 'deep blue sea' of curved space."

Wolf probes this strange middle realm in his recent work *The Dreaming Universe*, an exploration of the ever-shifting borderland between objective and subjective, material and mental realities. He wonders if the phenomenal reports of near-death experiences or UFO sightings may be occurrences of "a collective intent" happening in individuals as "big dreams." These dreams may reveal the existence of another realm, possibly a parallel realm that may have some objectivity, as is suggested by the physical evidence in several UFO reports. But he views the remarkable sightings as a "*visual* phenomenon, not a material phenomenon," consisting of "real images, not of real objects." The roots of the UFO and alien encounters may be in the quantum physical notion of observer-created reality. "Are we witnessing," he asks, "something akin to a 'big dream,' a survival dream of the human species that manifests in some of us?"

From the quantum perspective, alien encounters may be an experience of seeing *future images of ourselves* in the mirror of the unsettling faces of extraterrestrials, or in the mandala shapes of the strange aircraft. The extraordinary craft seen in the skies and the peculiar presences felt in our rooms may be *us*, or our descendants, returning from the future to haunt, console, advise, warn, or inspire us, or our own present desires for a new age.

The Time-Travel Hypothesis

"If there are other worlds parallel to ours, are all the doors closed?" Louis L'Amour once asked. "Or does one, here or there, stand ajar?"

From the whirling dervish perspective of quantum theory come mind-boggling possibilities for the origins and movement of UFOs. Michael D. Swords, professor of sciences at Western Michigan University, writes with great wit and verve about the world since Einstein in his essay on UFOs as time travelers in the September/October 1990 issue of *International UFO Reporter*.

Swords spins off "the good Prof. Einstein's" well-known special theory of relativity to point out that UFO phenomena may be "projections of consciousness, perhaps from other space and time dimensions into our reality." He entertains the possibility that science fiction and quantum physics may be helping us to understand how planet-hopping between stars and galaxies or even dream journeys may be accomplished by traveling through space warps, black holes, or worm holes in the universal fabric. As objects moving almost at the speed of light act as if they were leaving the space-time continuum, they may be entering *another* dimension of space-time, *another* space, *another* time.

This theory that objects go gallivanting in and out of the space-time continuum is just one of many presented as a resolution to one of the perplexing patterns in UFO reporting, that of the sudden in-and-out appearances of spacecraft and alien visitors.

There was a young girl named Bright
Whose speed was faster than light.
She went out one day
In a relative way
And came back the previous night.

—traditional limerick

The "three-tiered" flying saucer apparition captured in the McMinnville photograph is one bewildering illustration of this, as are the reports of entities materializing and dematerializing before startled witnesses. The theory also answers the cry that archskeptics inevitably give when they have their backs up against the debate wall: *they can't get here from there!* According to the time-travel scenario, there would be no time to take, no space to cross!

Conceding that time travel, as H. G. Wells proved, is a romantically tempting notion, especially since it would practically guarantee our own immortality, Swords still concludes that we should exercise enough restraint to be able to think clearly and humbly about the vast range of possible scenarios surrounding the UFO phenomenon.

On the other hand, he admits that maybe *none* of this is possible, "due to the insurmountable paradoxes that flitting about in time would cause." After all, he writes, "When it comes to reality we don't know what we're talking about."

The prolific author Brad Steiger doesn't completely dismiss the literal ET, or nuts-and-bolts, hypothesis. But in his recent book, *The Other*, he speculates that UFOs may very well be our cosmic neighbors living around the corner from us in the next cosmic continuum. "I don't know whether the children who see themselves in a spaceship or in Tibet actually go to Tibet or a spaceship as we know it," he admits. "But I think it is possible that the power of thought allows them to create a place, not an imaginary place, but a place that is as real to them as reality."

> *"The alien experience may be the collective experience of seeing your own future image in the mirror."*
> —Kenneth Ring

Jacques Vallee postulates in *Revelations*, his most recent study of the UFO phenomenon, an alternately intriguing idea that a kind of "nonhuman consciousness . . . manipulates space and time." He finds it curious that scientists who accept the idea of multiple universes and even some ufologists who accept the idea that "space-time could be folded to allow almost instantaneous travel from one point of our universe to another, still cling emotionally to the notion that any nonhuman form of consciousness is necessarily from outer space . . . the entities could be multidimensional beyond space-time itself. *They could even be fractal beings. The earth itself could be their home.*"

Angels and Aliens

Though some shadowy commentators have suggested that UFOs are demonic in origin, nature, and intent, it was none other than Billy Graham who said, "UFOs are astonishingly angel-like in some of their reported appearances."

In his luminous book *Angels: An Endangered Species*, Malcolm Godwin points out a passel of parallels between angels and aliens. Among them: both exist in inner and outer space and are superior beings by virtue of being closer to the Deity; they tend to be miraculously gifted in languages, speaking in the tongue of whatever land they visit; they are literally "messengers"; both use magic disks, wheels, or saucers as transportation; both are beings of light and radiate subtle auras; both convey serious

The levitation of St. Joseph of Copertino as depicted in an eighteenth-century drawing.

concern over the welfare of the people of our planet. Witness and witnessed seem cosmically bound together with a sense of mystic oneness.

143

Coincidences or correspondences? If true common ground between the two phenomena exists, how is it that there could be so many fascinating similarities between ancient and modern cosmic messengers? As part of his cross-cultural study of the uncanny pattern of descriptions of angels in cultures throughout the world, Godwin explores the elusive realm of subatomic particles.

"Not only are angels inseparable from God, they are also indivisible from their witness," he discov-

Artist's rendition of the common near-death experience of floating through a dark tunnel toward a bright light.

ered. "The angel, the ET or the UFO are inseparable from the individual who claims to have seen
them."

How is this so? Godwin asked. Those who pursue
the mysteries of quantum physics have discovered
that if "they expect a particle to act like a wave, it
does," Godwin concluded. "If they expect it to act
like a point, it likewise accommodates their idea."

The reason for this, as Heisenberg explained in
the principle named after him, is that any act of observation changes or alters the reality of what is
being observed. After Heisenberg, we've learned that
it is impossible to be objective, to "step outside of the
universe to observe it. We are part of our own exper-
iment."

Book Guide

Angels and Aliens
Keith Thompson (Addison-Wesley, 1988)

Angels: An Endangered Species
Malcolm Godwin (Simon & Schuster, 1990)

The Other
Brad Steiger (Inner Light Publications, 1992)

Parallel Universes
Fred Alan Wolf (Simon & Schuster, 1988)

Revelations
Jacques Vallee (Bantam Books, 1991)

Space-Age Pilgrimages and Skywatching Sites

The most beautiful thing we can experience is the mysterious. It is the source of all true art and science.

—Albert Einstein, *What I Believe*, 1930

Pilgrimage is the age-old tradition of making a journey to a legendary place or sacred shrine that binds people to a mythical past. In recent times this venerable practice has been revived. Just as we are struck by the opportunity to watch a "myth-in-the-making" by paying close attention to the UFO phenomenon, so too can we watch the mysterious process of "pilgrimage-sites-in-the-making." Thousands of people are now flocking to places around the world that have become famous because of reported sightings of flying saucers, suspicious military activity, or the promise of visitations by the Intergalactic Federation descending from the heavens.

Why would people take the trouble to venture so far on the strength of a newspaper story, television sound bite, or a tantalizing rumor?

Traditionally, the strong lure of the pilgrimage is the knowledge that some sites are considered to be powerfully different, even divine. Something happened on that ground, a god was encountered, a revelation handed down, a religion or sect founded, a mystery revealed—or promised to *soon* be revealed to the faithful. To journey there, to touch that ground, breathe that air, contemplate that story, is to venture to the "sacred center" in such a way that curious souls are able to affirm their own identity as a member of a specific religious or social tradition. It is a time-honored way to participate in a great mystery, a rite of passage that helps people move to the next stage of their lives, or inspires them to ponder the great range of human accomplishment.

> *"We find ourselves faced by powers which are far stronger than we had hitherto assumed, and whose base of operations is at present unknown to us."*
> —Dr. Wernher von Braun, 1959, on the deflection from orbit of a U.S. satellite

A brief list of the great pilgrimage sites might include Fatima, Portugal, where the Virgin Mary was allegedly seen by 80,000 people; Jerusalem's Wailing Wall, the last remnant of Solomon's Temple; the Black Stone at Mecca, site of Muhammad's ascension; the megalithic wonder at Stonehenge, symbol of the mystical power of ancient druids; Monet's gardens in Giverny, inspiration to thousands of art lovers; poet Emily Dickinson's home in Amherst; rock legend Jim Morrison's grave in Paris; the aboriginal entrance to the Dreamtime at Ayers Rock, Australia; or even Cooperstown, New York, the mythical birthplace of baseball.

In the modern UFO era, this deep urge to "go back to the source" for inspiration and revival by the mysterious powers of life has created pilgrimage sites out of many of the places associated with "first" sightings, first encounters or revelations with the Space Brothers, places that are shrouded in mystery and obscured by clandestine government doings. Other regularly visited areas are considered "windows," sites of regular and exciting observations of aerial phenomena, because they're believed to indicate "high strangeness" of possible UFO activity, signals of visiting craft from distant worlds that deserve diligent monitoring.

UFO Pilgrimage Sites and Hot Spots

Mount Rainier, Washington

Each year since Kenneth Arnold's legendary sighting of the nine flying disks skipping across the summit of Mount Rainier, UFO buffs have made the trek to the foot of the mountain. They gather to commemorate the event that marks the birth of the age of flying saucers, and maybe, through an exhibit of sheer faith, nudge along their return!

For over twenty-five years the New Age Foundation staged an annual UFO convention near the site. As Douglas Curran describes in his delightful book, *In Advance of the Landing,* the faithful gathered for several days before and after the June anniversary of Arnold's skybreaking report at a site they called SPLAASH, an acronym for the Spacecraft Protective Landing Area for Advancement of Science and Humanities. Site founder Wayne Aho formally declared to state and federal authorities that it was a *"free* Landing Zone" for both ETs and earthlings. Today, many still consider the site a "contact point" for the Space Brothers.

Other famed sightings in the Northwest include those at McMinnville, Oregon, near the Willamette River, in 1950 by Paul Trent and his wife. Their photographs of a shadowy domed craft have exhausted every sophisticated analysis, including NASA's computer enhancement tests. This area is still considered a UFO hot spot, as evidenced by a case that occurred in 1966 near Willamette Pass, Oregon, one for the

A 1950s skywatching photograph of five UFO researchers using a contemporary chart to help identify the myriad shapes that anomalous aerial phenomena take.

quantum physicists to ponder. A biochemistry professor snapped a reality-busting photograph of a classic flying saucer-shaped object in which "three images appear as one." Jenny Randles suggests the structured object may have appeared and reappeared in and out of reality in the split second the camera shutter was open. This bizarre possibility might account for the elusiveness of so many UFO observations, as quantum physicists theorize about subatomic "ghost" particles dancing in and out of unknown dimensions.

Yakima Indian Reservation

Just north of the Oregon border is another place regarded by some ufologists as a "window," or a site of frequent UFO flybys: Yakima, Washington. The airport at Yakima was Kenneth Arnold's destination on his day of infamy, and since the mid-1960s, the area has had myriad reports of blazing green fireballs and encounters with Bigfoot, aliens, and humanoids.

Only five miles south of Mount Rainier, Yakima Indian Reservation received 186 UFO reports between 1964 and 1984, most of them seen by fire lookouts. Their stories about strobing red-orange and white nocturnal lights and huge balls of light that stalk cars and trucks on back roads have inspired many investigations, including one organized by J. Allen Hynek. The resulting photographs of indistinct anomalous lights were inconclusive.

Because this is Indian land, anyone wishing to embark on a skywatching expedition should first seek permission and always treat the site with respect.

Mount Palomar Observatory, Southern California

George Adamski didn't just claim to take startling photographs of flying saucers descending after their long voyage from the planet Venus. On that legendary afternoon of November 20, 1952, he announced he had had the first meeting with one of their occupants. In his book coauthored with Desmond Leslie, *Flying Saucers Have Landed*, Adamski tried to set the interplanetary record straight. "Surface thinkers might like to conclude that I had a very original dream. Or that I may be out to make money for myself in the field of science fiction. I can assure such persons that nothing is farther from the truth."

Though his alleged revelations about the mysteries of Venus were squelched by the space program that would soon follow, Adamski's photographs inspired awe and his charismatic speaking style endeared him to a generation.

His followers still flock to the Palomar Gardens next to the observatory to celebrate their belief in Adamski as prophet and visionary because he was the first person to be contacted by extraterrestrial intelligence.

St. Paul, Alberta, Canada

In 1967, in honor of the Canadian Centennial, an unusual monument was constructed. At the site a sign proclaims:

> The area under the world's first UFO Landing Pad was designated international by the town of St. Paul as a symbol of our faith that mankind will maintain the outer universe free from national wars and strife. That future travel in space will be safe for all intergalactic beings. All visitors from Earth or otherwise are welcome to this territory and to the town of St. Paul.

While on a visit to receive a generous donation to her mission in 1982, Mother Teresa stood on the landing pad and quipped, "If there is sickness in outer space we would go there, too."

What to Do
If You See a UFO

The more of the following steps you can take, the more scientifically valuable your report will be:

1. Try and get another witness—as many other witnesses as possible.

2. If you have a camera handy, take as many pictures as possible. Don't worry about getting a "perfect" picture. Get as much background or foreground detail into the photo as possible.

3. Immediately after your sighting, make complete notes of everything you saw, all the details you can remember. Write down the appearance, color, motion, and size of the UFO, as well as what you were thinking and feeling when you had the experience. Write down the names and addresses of other witnesses.

4. If the UFO touched the ground, do what you can to protect the area—but don't disturb the area. Take photographs of the area to document it.

Most importantly,
report your UFO sighting.

Call the Center for UFO Studies any day of the week, any time of the day or night, at 312/271–3611. There are no regular hours; if no one is at the office, leave a message on the recorder. An investigator will contact you as soon as possible.

—Reprinted with permission of CUFOS, the J. Allen Hynek Center for UFO Studies

El Cajon, California

On the outskirts of San Diego, California, is the headquarters of the Unarius Foundation, founded by the late Ruth Norman, known in some circles as Uriel. The charismatic leader believed she had astrally traveled to more than sixty planets and received telepathic messages from the Space Brothers. After one startling conversation, she had a vision that a flotilla of thirty-three starships from the Interplanetary Confederation would land in San Diego in 2001, reportedly to help us solve any problems we have at that time.

The rest of her life was dedicated to helping the world prepare for the arrival of the saucers. In 1967 the Space Brothers convinced her to build an appropriate landing site for their fleet, and to get ready for the prodigious event she bought sixty-seven acres in nearby Jamul.

After several highly publicized and exuberantly attended landing parties failed to lure the Space Brothers, she decided instead to hold annual UFO conventions. Called Conclaves of Light, the gatherings feature processions of ufolks in "reincarnation" costumes, film screenings, and video lectures by Uriel on the virtues of universal love. They continue to attract the faithful with messages of love and hope for the dawning of the New Age of the Unarius Universe.

On the empty UFO landing site located in the scruffy foothills near Jamul, an old wooden sign with bright yellow letters still beckons to the heavens: WELCOME SPACE BROTHERS!

Roswell, New Mexico

The Roswell incident has the three-act structure of a great mystery novel: the Crash, the Cover-up, and the Investigation. After the high-profile incident was virtually buried by a stern Air Force pronouncement that the strange metallic debris discovered by

Mac Brazel was only a newfangled weather balloon, the case was laid to rest for the next thirty years.

The dramatic third act began to unfold in 1980 when William Moore and Charles Berlitz published the first exposé, *The Roswell Incident*, which rekindled the mystery. Though inaccurate in parts, the book sent a shock wave through the old Roswell community, compelling many of those involved to tell their stories for the first time. It also revived a question long on everybody's mind: If there have been thousands of reconnaissance missions from distant worlds, why hasn't at least one of their craft ever crashed? Surely the safety record of even advanced civilizations isn't perfect!

Throughout the 1980s investigations flourished, turning up witnesses and suppressed reports, all alluding to a massive cover-up. In the early 1990s, nuclear physicist and UFO researcher Stanton

Map of the Corona crash site, seventy miles north of Roswell.

Friedman teamed up with aviation writer Don Berliner to publish their conclusions in *Crash at Corona*. Investigators Kevin Randle and Donald Schmitt published their results in 1994 after combing through government and military records and interviewing over 350 witnesses, in a book called *The Truth about the UFO Crash at Roswell*.

Because the claim that there was an actual "crash retrieval" is far more dramatic than others, the ante is upped as far as hard evidence goes. Rumors are no longer enough. Still, the very word *Roswell* has taken on mystical overtones in the UFO movement because it symbolizes virtually everything that touches on the phenomenon: saucers, crashes, aliens, cover-up, the possibility that the truth could change everything. The UFO case of the century is still riddled with questions that stir deep emotions:

1. If the wreckage debris was only the scattered remains of a weather balloon, why was Brazel incarcerated for several days and convinced never to speak of the incident again, not even to his family?

2. If the aircraft was only one of the balloons sent up daily by the airfield, why was a Roswell radio station, KSWS, interrupted in the middle of its broadcast on the capture of a flying disk with an apocalyptic Teletype message: "Do not transmit. Repeat. Do not transmit this message. Stop communication immediately."

3. If the aliens did crash, why were they here? Did they have a message for us? Did any survive?

4. Because there is no precedent for the military to be so secretive about mere weather devices, and if the wreckage debris was not that of a spacecraft from another planet, then what was it? A top secret weapon from Russia, Japan, or America?

"Our lives will never be the same."
—Mac Brazel to Frank Joyce, a reporter with Roswell radio station KGFL, July 8, 1947

How Do You Prove This Stuff to a Skeptic?

157

"I was interviewed not long ago by an Austrian journalist. He put a question to me that could apply to most of the UFO/ET/New Age movement in all its forms: 'How do you prove any of this stuff to a skeptic?' The obvious answer, of course, is that you don't. A person has to have had some kind of direct, eye-opening, convincing personal experience to be transformed overnight from a devout scoffer to a devout believer.

"I have had moments of great glee when someone who had previously regarded me as more than slightly crazy rushed up to me and exclaimed, wide-eyed, with hand on my arm, 'My God! Have I got to tell you what happened to me last night!'"

—Tom Dongo, *The Alien Tide*

Roswell Update

On September 8, 1994, the Air Force finally submitted to years of petitions by the press, politicians, and Roswell conspiracy pundits by announcing the completion of a study they hoped would be the "final word on the subject." The AP story began:

Air Force Rejects UFO Theory in 1947 Roswell Incident.

A supposed alien spacecraft discovered near Roswell, N.M., 47 years ago likely was a secret Army Air Force balloon designed to monitor Soviet nuclear testing.

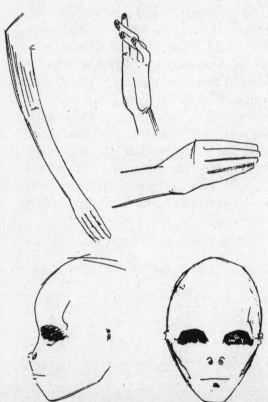

Drawings courtesy of Glenn Davis

Sketches by Glenn Davis, a Roswell mortician who worked at the hospital on Roswell Army Air Field, based on drawings by a nurse who allegedly saw four alien bodies there after the crash in July 1947.

Roswell's
UFO Museums

The International UFO Museum and Research Center

400–402 North Main, P.O. Box 2221
Roswell, NM 88202
505/625–9495
Daily 1 P.M. to 5 P.M.
Admission is free.

Recent coverage of the alleged 1947 saucer crash near Roswell has attracted more than 100,000 ufonatics to the museum since it opened its doors in 1992. In addition to a library, UFO exhibits, a video-viewing room, and a gift shop, there's an "operating room" modeled after the one in the movie *Roswell: The UFO Cover-up*, complete with an ET crash victim.

Outa Limits UFO Enigma Museum

6108 South Main, P.O. Box 6047
Roswell, NM 88202-6047
505/347–2275
Monday through Saturday 10 A.M. to 5 P.M.
Admission: $1 for adults, 50 cents for children.

There's a large video-viewing area and a few displays, but the big draw here is a marvelous re-creation of the crash site, complete with strobing blue lights, dummies of the alien casualties, and military guards. The staff has information on tours to the crash site.

You Are Not Alone

A 1990 Gallup Poll found that:

47% believe UFOs are "real"

46% believe intelligent life exists in outer space

30% believe that UFOs can be found in "imagination"

27% believe that UFOs have actually touched down and visited Earth

14% have seen a UFO

Quick UFO Facts

For every fundamentalist Christian there are five UFO believers

UFO believers outnumber Roman Catholics by a ratio of better than two to one

UFO believers outnumber the voters who placed Reagan, Bush, and Clinton in office

There are three adult Americans who believe that UFOs are real for every two skeptics

—*CUFOS Journal* analysis of the 1990 Gallup Poll

Rejecting all theories of aliens and UFOs, the Air Force said that contrary claims in sensational books and films are "undocumented, taken out of context, self-serving or otherwise dubious."

Instead, wrote Colonel Richard Weaver, author of the report, "The most likely source of the wreckage . . . was from Project Mogul balloon trains."

During a period of intense government sensitivity over the issue of atomic weapons, Mogul was a top secret project designed to launch weather balloons with sensing devices for monitoring atmospheric radioactivity. With the U.S. government so concerned that its monopoly on nuclear weapons might be threatened, any evidence of Soviet nuclear tests would have triggered a feverish search-and-recover mission.

Despite the government's pronouncement, ufologists are adamant that secrets persist. Roswell continues to be the hottest topic of debate in UFO circles.

The Flying Saucer Fever

The combined impact of three Roswell books, the 1993 Showtime movie *Roswell: The UFO Cover-up*, and a constant stream of investigators to the area has put Roswell on the UFO tourist map. Two museums there are dedicated to the UFO phenomenon: the downtown International UFO Museum and Research Center, and the Outa Limits UFO Enigma Museum, located in the shadows of the old Army Air Field on the outskirts of town. Between them, the two facilities have attracted 100,000 visitors from around the world since opening in 1992.

John Price is the gracious curator and official guide of the

"While we may all agree the Cold War is over, I think we can also agree that this nation must continue to maintain tight security on certain military projects."

—Air Force Colonel Douglas J. Kennett to *Popular Science*, March 1994

Billy Meier
Pleiadean

The tale of Eduard "Billy" Meier occupies a limbo region in the UFO cosmology. After nearly twenty years of debate over the most impressive photographs from a most unlikely source, a Swiss farmer named Billy Meier, questions remain. Is Meier an opportunist or, as he claims, one of the Chosen? Are his photos authentic or the work of an elaborate hoax team? Silver disks and beamships? And who is the 330-year-old seductress named Semjase from the planet Erra in the Pleiades, the Seven Sisters cluster of many an ancient mythology?

Inspired by a series of sensational newspaper and magazine articles during the summer and fall of 1976, hundreds of visitors began making a pilgrimage to the village of Hinwil in southeast Switzerland. Their mission: to visit a forty-eight-year-old one-armed illiterate, a visionary caretaker named Billy Meier.

Meier was already considered eccentric by his neighbors for his habit of disappearing for hours or days at a time into the nearby forests. Then he began to emerge with spectacular photographs of spaceships, which were being published around the world alongside Meier's supporting stories of reputed contacts with an advanced race of beautiful, long-haired ETs from the distant Pleiades constellation.

How did these alien beings traverse that great galactic highway? Meier's guide, Semjase, had a tentative answer. Starships from the Pleiades, she confided to him, used a propulsion system that allowed them to break the speed-of-light barrier and

and the Connection

163

travel the 500-million-mile distance in seven hours.

Physics aside, Meier's own worst critics admit that the photographs, "even if fakes, are remarkably clever." William Spaulding's Ground Saucer Watch technology group investigated some of the photographs with computer enhancement and apparently detected string holding up models, although test results are inconclusive.

The possibility that this was "the most infamous hoax in ufology," as it was called in the December 1980 *MUFON Journal*, only led to further questions: How can a one-armed man hold up a model and snap a photograph? Why would he?

Whatever Meier's motives might be, his photographs have magically captured the imagination of millions who see in the golden auras surrounding his beamships the entire mystery of the UFO phenomenon.

Photo courtesy of Genesis III and Lee Elders

"The Sunlight Scene," a classic photo of a Pleiadean beamship taken by Eduard "Billy" Meier on March 29, 1976, at Hasenbol, Switzerland.

UFO Enigma Museum, which features wall charts, photographs of flying disks from around the world, video displays, drawings by schoolkids, and a panoramic exhibit of the crashed saucer scene that Mac Brazel discovered.

Price told me that he gets great pleasure from watching the looks of delight on the faces of his guests, especially the skeptics.

"People want to see the light. After seeing our exhibits, even the skeptics will admit that there may be something to it. There's just something about the Roswell incident that opens up a new part of them, even if they didn't know they were interested in UFOs before. But at our museum they can at least see a possibility of something they thought existed only in science fiction or fairy tales. They're able to visualize UFOs for the first time. People have seen so much science fiction become reality that the idea of UFOs or saucers or aliens isn't too hard to believe in anymore. You know, what this tells you is that there's no end to the mysteries of science or the universe."

Groom Lake, Nevada

They call it The Ranch, The Box, Watertown Strip, The Pig Farm, and Dreamland. But in honor of old government maps and the sheer mystifying ring of it, most people know it as "Area 51" of the Nevada Test Site.

Courtesy of the Smithsonian Institution

U.S. Air Force B-2 Stealth Bomber, secretly test-flown at Area 51, is "invisible" on radar screens.

Located near a vast lake bed 140 miles north of Las Vegas, it's a "remote test facility," as the U.S. Air Force officially refers to it. The Base That Doesn't Exist is comprised of hangars, barracks, colossal parabolic antennae, radar, test planes, what is reputedly the world's longest paved runway, and the world's hottest test pilots.

In such a vacuum of information, curiosity, if not paranoia, runs rampant. In 1954 it was a secret air base, convenient to the Atomic Energy Commission's nuclear bomb testing area at White Sands. This is where the U-2, SR-71, and F-117A spy planes were tested in absolute secrecy. Since then, intrepid travelers have made the rugged trip to the desert to witness the thunderous air shows provided by F-15s, F-16s, B-52s, the Russian Sukhoi Su-22 and MiG-23, and, rumors have it, the test flights of reputed spy planes like the *Aurora*, regarded by *Aviation Week & Space Technology* magazine as a "quantum leap in aviation." Of the announced 1994 defense budget of $84.1 billion, $14.3 billion—the equivalent of the entire NASA annual budget—was procured for secret or "black" programs like these.

But that's not why Area 51 is fast becoming the most popular skywatching site in America.

The one and only meeting place for UFO buffs, military personnel, and stray tourists: Pat and Joe Travis's "world famous" Little A'Le'Inn, in Rachel, Nevada.

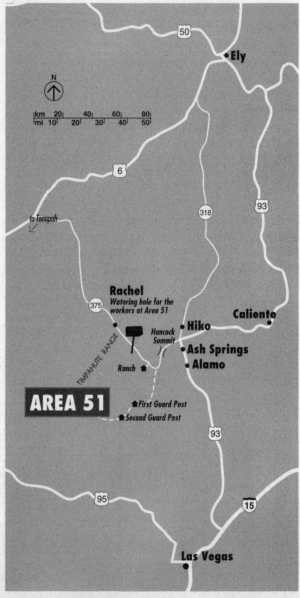

Map of the Area 51 quadrant of a highly secret military base at the Nevada Test Site, north of Las Vegas.

On any given day in the town of Rachel at Pat and Joe Travis's legendary Little A'Le'Inn, a café festooned with wild and wacky UFO memorabilia, you will find UFO buffs, film crews, conspiracy mongers, skeptical journalists, aviation lovers, military gadflies who call themselves the Dreamland Interceptors, and even a few pop-eyed folks who call *themselves* aliens. These pilgrims flock here from around the world to hold vigil and view the *lights*.

The Rumors of Hidden Saucers

In 1989 an enigmatic man named Bob Lazar, a self-proclaimed physicist, announced on television that he had been working at a hush-hush base at S4, a Nellis Range base far more secret than Area 51. According to Lazar, flying saucers are being hidden in nine underground hangars at S4, and the government is replicating them using a process called "back engineering." His scientific analysis of the actual mechanics of spacecraft dazzles some, while drawing sighs and shrugs from others.

As the deductive investigator Glenn Campbell says, likening the Area 51 puzzle to a Sherlock Holmes story, "The setting is real, just like Baker Street, and there is an intellectual challenge in following the clues."

Consciously or not, Lazar's descriptions of having seen and worked on a "sport model" saucer sounded like something out of a James Bond movie, especially the jargon about "anti-gravity" engines and wobbly-legged aliens acting as advisers in the shadows of underground hangars and a back engineering program that would allow the government to learn from our distant engineer cousins.

Lazar's story immediately captured the attention of the "nuts-and-bolts" enthusiasts eager to finally have evidence of a downed saucer at a secret military facility. Every legend needs a landmark, so a simple rancher's mailbox forlornly stuck in the ground at mile marker LN 29.5 on Nevada State Highway 375 has become the "X" that marks this tale's treasure. The black mailbox serves notice as the closest spot the average UFO enthusiast can come to viewing the distant complex of military buildings and the nearby nightly light show of silhouetted diamond- and boomerang-shaped aircraft. In short, it's become one of *the* pilgrimage sites for avid UFO buffs from around the world who hope to see flying saucers that they believe are here to spy on or keep watch over one of the most secret military bases on earth.

After years of skywatching over Area 51, local military watchdog Glenn Campbell concludes, "I've never seen anything I couldn't explain, just a lot of military activity that could look like saucers if you're in that frame of mind." Apparently many folks are. Campbell goes on to say that the area now attracts "tours, conferences, believers, skeptics, and charlatans, not to mention a steady stream of urban pilgrims in search of enlightenment." Some arrive at night and drive or hike on the remote back roads, unaware of or ignoring the signs that

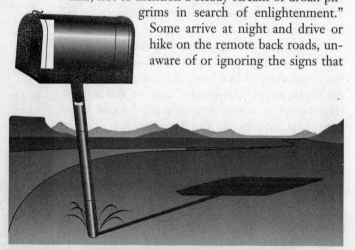

The infamous black mailbox near Rachel, Nevada, meeting point for skywatchers from around the world who come to scan the skies over Area 51.

OMNI Magazine Asks: What Would You Say to an Alien?

"Get out! Go back! Save yourselves! You don't know what you're getting into. Prolonged contact with our species can only degrade your present standards, whatever they are."
—George Carlin, comedian

"Please don't reveal this is your first visit or you will break the hearts of thousands of UFO believers."
—Philip J. Klass, UFO debunker and contributing editor to *Aviation Week* magazine

"Welcome—we hope you find us peaceful, too. . . . We always believed you were out there! Would you like some champagne and caviar to celebrate your arrival? Then we have a million questions to ask you. . . . And did you see E.T.?"
—Robin Leach, host of *Lifestyles of the Rich and Famous*

"I don't mean to be too sensible or realistic, but I doubt I would be able to get anyplace near the peaceful extraterrestrials who visited Earth. They would immediately be snapped up by Hard Copy, Prime Time, 20/20, I.C.M., Creative Artists, and other talent agencies, . . .
—Helen Gurley Brown, editor of *Cosmopolitan*

"Due to language barriers and other sociological considerations, it is highly unlikely that we will have any success with verbal communications. I have therefore handed the assignment to my friend Spock, who is highly skilled in nonverbal diplomacy."
—Leonard Nimoy, actor and director

From *OMNI*, January 1995 (Used with permission)

warn: "Use of Deadly Force Authorized." They risk arrest and expensive fines, if not physical harm. What can be seen at the black mailbox? On a typical skywatching night it is common to see the landing lights of airliners en route to Vegas. Several times a night, unmarked Black Hawk helicopters buzz the hills and back roads looking for trespassers. Other ominous craft hover motionlessly in the sky, secret military planes painted in dark camouflage with their running lights turned off.

Alone under the incandescent stars with only the sound of the wind blowing across the cactus-punctuated desert, the lights of the distant base make the blood race. Every movement in the heavens and on earth seem full of meaning and glory. This is a land of destructive schemes beyond most imaginations, but also a land where dreams learn to fly.

The *"Area 51" Viewers Guide* has maps, milepost logs, and lots of practical information for visitors in search of mysterious aircraft. The *Groom Lake Desert Rat* newsletter is dedicated to keeping tabs on any activity in the area. Both can be ordered from creator Glenn Campbell, HCR, P.O. Box 38, Rachel, NV 89001 (Internet e-mail address: psychospy@aol.com).

Giant Rock, California

"My whole body was shaken up when the Council of Seven Lights came through," wrote George Van Tassel, the space-age prophet, of his 1953 contact with an extraterrestrial in the golden-green mist at Giant Rock, an ancient Indian holy site near Joshua Tree.

What began as a small group of curiosity seekers who gathered for Saturday night meetings in the shadow of the Giant Rock to listen to Van Tassel's channeled messages from the ETs grew into veritable conventions. The first annual Giant Rock Space Convention in 1954 lured more than 5,000 people clamoring to witness a possible visitation of the UFOs that Van Tassel proclaimed he had been in contact with.

After a being named Solganda telepathically informed Van Tassel that the biggest difference between them and us was age, the Space Brothers told him how to build the four-story-high, dome-shaped Integraton, his longevity machine. He regarded the plans for this "electrostatic magnetic generator" as a twenty-first-century tabernacle for Moses. His Forever Young machine, alas, turned out to be forever in need of funds.

"This is a method to a fuller, longer, energetic life for everybody," Van Tassel once said. Thousands gathered annually at the Giant Rock for conventions in honor of Van Tassel until 1977, many holding out hope for the resuscitation of the rejuvenation machine. But when he died in 1978, the dream machine was, according to his estimates, about 88 percent complete.

The Integraton is still at Giant Rock, attracting seekers of all beliefs from throughout the world.

Gulf Breeze, Florida

Since the mid-1980s, unexplained sonic booms, skyquakes, and crop circles have been reported along the white sand beaches of Gulf Breeze, Florida, across the sandbar from Pensacola. In November 1987 Ed Walters snapped five Polaroid photographs of alleged flying saucers cruising over his home. The moment he took the fifth photo he was "paralyzed" by a blue beam that lifted him in the air and almost choked him. A telepathic message came to him in a sensation similar to that of flipping through the pages of a book.

When Walters mailed his photographs to the *Gulf Breeze Sentinel*, the paper's editor learned from his mother and others that they had also observed a UFO similar to the one Walters had captured on film.

For the next several months, Walters took dozens of UFO photographs and had repeated scrapes with what he believed to be aliens. His subsequent book,

The Gulf Breeze Sightings, coauthored with his wife, Frances, was released to great notoriety in 1990. Hoax charges were leveled, but official UFO organizations also came to his defense, and the book's status among ufologists continues to be controversial. Some investigators speculated that the lights were naval flares, noctilucent clouds, jet streams, or pulsing satellites.

Whatever the source, the skies teem with thought-provoking lights. The white sand beaches have become one of the most popular skywatching sites in America, on some nights drawing dozens of people with their arsenal of binoculars, telescopes, cameras, and sound recorders, as they wait till the midnight hour to witness the dancing lights of craft from outer space.

Sedona, Arizona

Sedona's earth magic was known to Native Americans for millennia. Recently, it has come to be symbolized by the "vortex" phenomenon, described by local writer Alan Leon as "a gushing geyser of natural Earth energies." The red rock canyons of Sedona hold an undeniable power. Each year thousands of people come to experience its healing powers and geological wonders, drawn by Native American lore surrounding its eighty archaeological sites and by the ancient spirits of the canyons. In the past few years, these visits have become more like pilgrimages or quests as the area has been transformed into a mecca for spiritual warriors intent on Magical Mystery Tours of personal growth, a "metaphysical refuge," as Tom Dongo, another Sedona writer, describes it, "where people can explore any realm of human consciousness without fear of ridicule." Many people venture to Sedona because it has become, as Dongo adds, "one of the world's hot spots for UFO activity."

One typical report of a bizarre sighting occurred on November 26, 1991, when two men watched a "metallic glint in the sky over Secret Canyon" and

Vortex Centers and Other Earth Magic

173

Those who study the theory of vortex energy believe that there are approximately twenty-two vortex centers around the world. Major vortex centers would include megalithic sites such as Stonehenge, Newgrange, Malta, and Easter Island, and religious centers such as Angkor Wat, Machu Picchu, the City of Refuge, the Great Pyramid, the North and South Poles, and Sedona.

What is behind the Sedona vortex enigma? Geologists will tell you it's simply the basalt layers under the red rocks, which have a high iron oxide content, lending the area a magnetic quality. This in turn is interpreted by others as having an influence on paranormal activity. Ufolks say UFOs and ETs are magnetically drawn to red rocks.

Vortex Resources

The Mysteries of Sedona
Tom Dongo (Hummingbird Publishing, 1993)

Sedona UFO Connection
Richard Dannelley (Vortex Society, 1993)

Sedona Vortex Guidebook
(Light Technology Publishing, 1991)

Vortex Society
P.O. Box 948, Sedona, AZ 86339

174

The Aetherius Society

One UFO group that walks its talk is the still-flourishing Aetherius Society. It was founded in 1954 by George King, a London taxi driver who claimed to have been contacted by the Cosmic Intelligence and instructed to prepare himself to become the Voice of Interplanetary Parliament. His society acts as a medium between earthlings and the cosmic masters, and King teaches that thought and prayer can be focused on the world's problem spots. His followers still gather to charge and store spiritual energy in "prayer batteries," which are often carried on long treks up summits such as Mount Kilimanjaro, so the energy can be beamed out across the world. Not unlike cloistered monks, society members believe their prayer power has helped avert major catastrophes, including interstellar warfare and earthquakes.

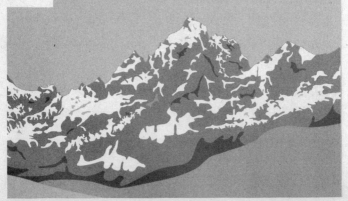

observed for over ten minutes as the craft "bounced and wobbled slightly like boats anchored in rough water." Dongo postulates that this odd sight was caused by UFOs riding on Earth's magnetic fields, giving the appearance of boats sitting on undulating water.

So potent are the natural forces around Sedona that certain myths about the area are gaining popularity: that it was the site of ancient Lemuria, or will be the next Tibet, or at the very least become one of the important "contact areas" between Earth and the extraterrestrials.

Sand Dunes State Forest, Minnesota

In 1992 Elk River, Minnesota, had a rash of UFO sightings. Since then, Stephen Greer, an emergency-room physician from Asheville, North Carolina, has organized nighttime skywatches at the William T. Cox Diamond Anniversary Unit of Sand Dunes State Forest. Greer is a practicing ufologist who believes in benevolent visitors. He is avidly attempting to add a new level to the classic four close encounter categories established by J. Allen Hynek. For Greer, a CE-5 will be a "human-initiated contact with aliens."

As reported by Alex Heard in *Outside* magazine, Greer founded CSETI (The Center for the Study of Extraterrestrial Intelligence) in Minneapolis in 1990. Believing that we not only shouldn't wait for Godot or for UFOs but should actually initiate contact, he leads skywatching groups that are equipped like a Star Trek expedition with a New Age "hardware cornucopia" that includes high-power halogen lights, radar detectors, walkie-talkies, and the full range of cameras. Membership in CSETI hovers around 1,000. Besides holding group meetings, they also travel to UFO hot spots around the country, accumulating evidence and attempting to trigger alien contact.

Gallup Poll

Q **Have you, yourself, ever seen anything you thought was a UFO?**

	1973	1978	1990
Yes	11%	9%	14%
No	89%	91%	85%
No opinion	*	*	1%

*Less than 0.5%

Q **Do you think there are people somewhat like ourselves living on other planets in the universe, or not?**

	1973	1978	1989	1990
Yes	48%	51%	41%	46%
No	38%	33%	48%	36%
No opinion	16%	16%	11%	18%

Source: The Gallup Organization (U.S.A.)

More UFO Museums

The Flying Saucer Museum
909 Linden Street
Allentown, PA 18102
Guided tours are available.

**UFO/ET World Museum &
Scientific Research Library**
P.O. Box 4533
Trenton, NJ 08611
609/888–1358
Not a standing exhibit, this organization will rent its
museum space to groups.

Book Guide

The Alien Tide
Tom Dongo (Hummingbird Publishing, 1990)

Crash at Corona
Stanton T. Friedman and Don Berliner
(Marlowe & Company, 1994)

The Gulf Breeze Sightings
Ed Walters and Frances Walters (Avon Books, 1991)

Light Years: An Investigation into the Extra-terrestrial Experiences of Eduard Meier
Gary Kinder (The Atlantic Monthly Press, 1987)

Roswell in Perspective
Karl Pflock (Fund for UFO Research: P.O. Box 277,
Mount Rainier, MD 20712; 1994)

The Truth about the UFO Crash at Roswell
Kevin D. Randle and Donald R. Schmitt
(M. Evans and Company, 1994)

The Truth
Is Out There

You unlock this door with the key of imagination. Beyond it is another dimension, a dimension of sound, a dimension of sight, a dimension of mind. You're moving into a land of both shadow and substance, of things and ideas. You've just crossed over . . . into the Twilight Zone.

—Rod Serling

Rod Serling, the creative genius behind the popular 1960s television show *The Twilight Zone*, said he knew they had "arrived" when he learned that Secretary of State Dean Rusk had used the show's title in a speech to describe the peculiar world of diplomacy.

Thirty years later the very words "The Twilight Zone," along with the otherworldly music from the opening sequence, are instantly understood by most Americans as a vivid description of the undeniable *strangeness*, the quirkiness, of the world.

For five years and 156 episodes, Serling uncannily captured the corrosive sense of alienation in postwar America, and the creeping realization that nothing in the twilight realm is quite as it seems. With exquisite panic and delicious fear, we were told over and over that we were *on our own*. In Serling's words, "The worst fear of all is the fear of the unknown working on you, which you cannot share with others. . . ." That fear of the unknown was a mask with a thousand faces pulled back again and again to reveal the threat of nuclear war, scientific experiments run amok, and the eerie sense of being watched that led to doubts of one's own identity. Yet these anxieties were somehow relieved by entering "the zone" every Friday night. Through Serling's starkly vivid, richly imaginative stories, a remarkable window into America was thrown open, an uncanny stage on which the bewildering themes swirling around the UFO phenomenon were portrayed.

181

Each question about *them*, the alien presence, was reflected in themes touching on the soullessness of an increasingly robotic world, the fear of strangers living next door, the terror felt by marooned astronauts, the confusion of time travel, the euphoria of parallel universes, and the distrust for the spiritually corrosive aspects of science and technology. Discussing the elaborate plotlines and exhilarating twisted endings became a kind of secret handshake, a wink to those who knew, as Serling intoned in the epilogue to "The Last Flight" episode, that "There are more things in heaven and earth, and in the sky, than perhaps *can* be dreamt of. And somewhere in between heaven, the sky, the earth, lies the Twilight Zone."

And yet the series had a simple message that cut through the angst of the times. As Marc Scott Zicree has written in his definitive companion book to the series, the basic message of the show was that, "The only escape from alienation lies in reaching out to others, trusting in their common humanity. Give in to the fear and you are lost." There was a new and daring magic in this portrayal of the odd and quirky twists of the postwar UFO-era America, one in which, as Mario Vargas Llosa writes, "Strange is a holy word."

It's No Wonder

The way the world keeps getting demystified, it's no wonder there's so little wonder left. As British scientific gadfly Bryan Appleyard has written, the message now is that there's "nothing special about what the universe looks like from a human-sized perspective. In short, nothing special about us." Other recent fly-in-the-ointment theories claim that the soul is noth-

> "The time will have to come when we realize that we're not the center of the universe. The galaxy may be teeming with life. There may be millions of civilizations."
> —Richard Terrile, astronomer at the Jet Propulsion Laboratory

ing more than a few random synapse firings in the brain and dreams are simply electrical pulses in the central nervous system. A famous astronomer wrote in his study of the Big Bang with cold logic, "The more the universe seems comprehensible, the more it also seems pointless. There is no solace in the fruits of our research."

If the traditional sources of solace aren't enough anymore, where do we turn for the inspiration and the courage to face the uncertain future? How can we fight the "war against the imagination," as one poet so powerfully described the battle of the 1960s?

In the 1920s Parisian artists called it "nostalgia for the future," as if to say, we long for what we used to think the world would be!

With such anxiety about the unknown running rampant in our times, more and more people are turning to the realm of fantasy and science (or speculative) fiction, which has been described as "future memory," not just escapism, but access to a vigorous and optimistic vision of the coming times.

Imagine, If You Will

In what could be called a *Twilight Zone* for the millennium, *The X-Files* has achieved cult status after only two years on the air. And just as *The Twilight*

Photo courtesy of Paramount Pictures

Cast of television's *Star Trek: The Next Generation*, 1994.

183

Zone had its tagline, "Imagine if you will," *The X-Files* has its buzz phrase: "The truth is out there." The themes of the two shows are vastly different, illustrating how our culture's attitude toward authority and science has changed over two decades.

The Twilight Zone depicted the paranormal as a hidden menace lurking behind white picket fences or underneath the visor of a malt shop attendant. On *The X-Files* it's no great revelation that life has its surreal sides; it's taken for granted and played hauntingly straight. The overriding wisdom of the show is a form of self-preservation: *trust no one* in a world where the "bizarre is real."

Although the source material for the show comes out of the imagination of its creator, Chris Carter, many episodes seem to be inspired by some of the most notorious stories in the real UFO files, the more unexplained the better. This is befitting of the times, as even one Hollywood producer admits that "there's an exploding fascination with anything science can't explain."

"Trust no one," were the famous last words of the first season, uttered by an expiring informant named Deep Throat. The simple warning encapsulates the great appeal of the show and plays to the increasing paranoia and cynicism about such established institutions as the government and the media. Concepts revolving around covert U.S. military operations and disinformation, as well as secretive information on the status of intergalactic visitors and their retrieved spacecraft, are titillating for viewers.

Like *The Twilight Zone*, *The X-Files* cleverly feeds on this distrust of authority, not contributing to the paranoia, but encouraging people to think for themselves. In an innovative move, the main

> "It's been said that science fiction and fantasy are two different things: science fiction, the improbable made possible; fantasy, the impossible made probable."
> —Rod Serling

184

Ten Modern UFO

> *"We're living in a science-fiction time. We're swimming in an ocean of technology, and that's why* Star Trek, Star Wars, *and 90% of the most successful films of the last 10 years are science fiction."*
> —Ray Bradbury, *Time*, November 28, 1994

2001: A Space Odyssey (1968)

Stanley Kubrick's adaptation of Arthur C. Clarke's short story "The Sentinel" stands out like the polestar in the night sky of movie history. Like any great work of art it is inexhaustibly complex and invites repeated viewings. The mystery hovers around the central image of a monolith that was left behind by aliens four million years ago to either trigger evolution at crisis points in human history or send a signal to our early "visitors" when humans reached a new level of technological sophistication. Each time the black slab appears and the haunting soundtrack hums on, as during the prehistoric ape-men scenes, or when the astronauts discover it on the moon, the viewer's imagination is electrified by the implications of the mystery of how our species made each giant leap of consciousness. Was it a quirk of nature? Or were we nudged along by extraterrestrial overseers? The monolith last appears at the deathbed of an astronaut who has ventured to Jupiter, and then suddenly we are back in space watching a "starchild" floating in the embryonic fluid of space, appearing one moment like the alien drawn by hundreds of abductees, and the next like an angel hovering above all creation. Sheer dreamtime.

and Space Classics

Star Wars (1977)

Who can forget the first time they saw *Star Wars*? More than just dazzling and unprecedented special effects, George Lucas's romp through the galaxy in a junkyard spaceship touched the whole world through its sheer exuberance about our future in the stars. Flat-earthers and anti-space-travel spoil-sports were left behind at the spaceport. The classic futuristic fantasy features the white-robed hero, Luke Skywalker (Mark Hamill), the darkly villainous Darth Vader (the voice of James Earl Jones), the spunky royal Princess Leia (Carrie Fisher), the space cowboy Han Solo (Harrison Ford), the cool wizard Ben Obi-Wan Kenobi (Alec Guinness), droids R2D2 and C3PO, spaceships, fantastic alien planets, and a detonating Death Star. Any shivers left over from the fright-wig, rubber-masked sci-fi flicks of the 1950s were smoothed over by the unforgettable space saloon scene. Distant planets are demystified by the vision of jazz-loving hipster aliens and the disembodied mentor "Force." Together with its sequels, *The Empire Strikes Back* (1980) and *Return of the Jedi* (1983), Lucas's trilogy—part legend, part comic book, part fantasy—is now part of our cultural and future folklore.

Ten Modern UFO

Close Encounters of the Third Kind (1978)
Steven Spielberg's best storytelling. Richard Dreyfuss's character follows the arc of Joseph Campbell's hero journey model and finds his bliss inside the Mother (ship) of all UFOs. François Truffaut plays the mysterious investigator Lacombe (inspired by Jacques Vallee), Melinda Dillon plays a great hysteric, and Cary Guffey plays the Spielberg surrogate. When you wish upon a star, you might get a great movie—at least you get out of the suburbs.—R. Beban

Star Trek: The Motion Picture (1979),
Star Trek II: The Wrath of Khan (1982),
Star Trek III: The Search for Spock (1984),
Star Trek IV: The Voyage Home (1986),
Star Trek: The Final Frontier (1989),
Star Trek: The Next Generation (1994)
Not just a television series and a movie serial, *Star Trek* is a parallel universe populated by self-sufficient worlds with their own genealogy, customs, and languages. Just uttering the words "federation starfleet," "phaser," "holodeck," and "Beam me up, Scotty" brings pleasure to Trekkies that borders on euphoria. A mere seventy-nine episodes have spawned six movies and three spin-off series that are broadcast in seventy-five countries, not to mention massive conventions, best-selling books, and big revenues. *Star Trek's* popularity is a marvel of multicultural optimism about our future explorations into deep space, while provocatively asking what it will mean to be "human" among alien civilizations. The series keeps fueling the UFO phenomenon, reinvigorat-

and Space Classics

ing our vision of spacecraft, aliens, and the huge hovering question, "What would we do if we were there or they were here?" Captain Kirk, Dr. Spock, Scotty, Captain Picard, Data, Captain Janeway, and a cast of thousands of aliens have put a human face on the great unknown of the unexplored realms.

Alien (1979), **Aliens** (1986), **Alien 3** (1992)
Or "Ripley's Believe It or Not" expedition to a newly discovered but malevolent planet. In this Gothic horror trilogy played out on abandoned spaceships, Sigourney Weaver is the Amazon heroine Ripley, who defeats the repulsive alien life-forms lurking in every crevice of each episode. These are brilliantly crafted but unrelentingly horrifying visions of future space travel and the fate of colonists on distant worlds.

E.T. The Extra-Terrestrial (1982)
Chased away by paranoid U.S. authorities, an alien spaceship is forced to fly off, leaving behind an adorable alien, alone and frightened in suburbia. A sweet friendship unfolds between this wide-eyed, purring alien with telepathic and telekinetic powers and the fatherless ten-year-old boy named Eliot (Henry Thomas), who finds a mystery lurking for him in his own backyard. Steven Spielberg's compassionate script touches on the opportunism of federal agencies, magical shows of extraterrestrial powers, and the spellbinding portrayal of children who believe in the miracle of friendship. Directed by Spielberg, it's one of the highest grossing films of all time.

Ten Modern UFO

Repo Man (1984)

Writer/director Alex Cox creates the classic anti-heroic mentor movie, with Harry Dean Stanton as a deliciously sleazy Obi-Wan Kenobi, and Emilio Estevez as his Luke Skywalker. Watch out for the generic food and the Christmas tree car deodorizers. The Chevy Malibu with the radioactive trunk is just a big McGuffin (red herring), but the ending proves that it isn't just swamp gas that rises.
—R. B.

Starman (1984)

Responding to messages from a U.S. satellite inviting it to Earth, an alien's spacecraft is shot down by the Air Force. Really just a glowing orb of light, this Starman (Jeff Bridges) is forced to land in Wisconsin, where he magically shape-shifts into a dead ringer for a deceased house-painter. The old alien drop-in tale is transformed into an on-the-road love story between the uncanny birdlike visitor and the widow Jenny (Karen Allen), as they race the cosmic clock across the country to meet his ride home at Great Meteor Crater in Arizona.

and Space Classics

Uforia (1985)

See it for the sly, sardonic script, by director John Binder, and for the marvelous cast. Cindy Williams plays Arlene, the supermarket checker who believes in two things: UFOs and the fact that she needs a man. Versatile and sexy Fred Ward (in a pre–Henry Miller role) is the stud-muffin of Arlene's dreams, and Harry Dean Stanton (sleazy yet again) steals the picture as an alcoholic con man. The *National Enquirer* never had a better advertising reel.—R. B.

Fire in the Sky (1993)

On their way home from the forest, a group of loggers in Arizona's White Mountains spot a glowing orb of light just ahead in the trees. In what has become one of the most controversial and widely known abduction stories, Travis Walton (a convincing D. B. Sweeney) ventures out of the truck for a closer look and is struck by a ray of blue light and beamed aboard an alien craft. Missing for five days, he returns to tell a frightening tale that no one believes.

characters, agents Fox Muldur (David Duchovny) and Dana Scully (Gillian Anderson), actually work for the FBI, but they investigate fringe "X-File" cases, becoming believers of paranormal realities officially denied by all the powers that be. Through their adventures we become privy to the inside workings of government and are able to feel the vicarious thrills of their bizarre investigations into current phenomena, much of it swirling around the UFO/alien question. And like the ancient message that something vital is to be discovered on an epic journey, the motto that opens up each episode shines like the Holy Grail: the truth is out there and will set us free.

Unsolved Encounters

Echoing the sci-fi boom, triggered, many believe, by the approaching millennium, several television programs notable for featuring positive extraterrestrial- and UFO-related segments have appeared in the last few years, including syndicated magazine-style shows such as *Unsolved Mysteries*, *Sightings*, and *Encounters*. These "reality-based" shows are remarkable revealers of the shifting social attitude toward the paranormal, as they move to the "other side" of the debate. It is commonplace now to see segments on the latest rash of UFO sightings, people who claim to have encountered aliens and display physical scars, reports of NASA shuttle "encounters" with UFOs, and reports on the latest technology used to authenticate UFO photographs. By sidestepping the spiritual or mystical side of the paranormal phenomenon, these programs claim to stick to the hard facts.

Photo courtesy of Paramount Pictures

Leonard Nimoy as the Vulcan, Mr. Spock, in his 1994 guest appearance on *Star Trek: The Next Generation*.

Their common ancestor is the late-1970s classic *In Search Of*, a nonskeptical paranormal-friendly program hosted by Leonard Nimoy of *Star Trek* fame. For many viewers, this was their first foray into popular world mysteries such as reincarnation, Atlantis, the Loch Ness Monster, the Bermuda Triangle, and earth mysteries such as tornadoes, volcanoes, and earthquakes. *In Search Of* continues to run in syndication and can be credited with opening up a new generation to the exhilaration of thoughts and ideas outside the mainstream.

Channeling the Heavens: Contactees with a Message

In recent years there appears to have been a phenomenal rise in the number of people claiming to hear spirit voices. Some of the most popular "new consciousness" books available today are written by folks who believe they have channeled wisdom from extraterrestrials. Barbara Marciniak, author of *Bringers of the Dawn* and *Earth*, is a trance channel who spends most of her time traveling and lecturing on what she says extraterrestrials from the star system Pleiades have channeled through her. Bestselling author Ruth Montgomery has "Guides" who tell her that space travelers are now visiting earth "from places in the spectrum of galaxies beyond the

---

When the creator of the legendary television series The Twilight Zone *was asked how he thought of the title, Rod Serling remarked, "I thought I'd made it up, but I've heard that there is an Air Force term relating to a moment when a plane is coming down on approach and it cannot see the horizon, it's called the twilight zone."*

—*The Twilight Zone Companion*

Milky Way." Brad Steiger, an author on UFO and paranormal subjects whose books have sold more than fifteen million copies worldwide, insists that the "very survival of Planet Earth and the human species depends upon our ability to achieve a balance with the other . . . intelligence that exists beyond the UFO mystery." These channelers, along with many contactees, feel a great urgency to relay the messages that were given them by UFO occupants. Typically these messages are a call for world or intergalactic peace, and an urging for environmental awareness and caring for the earth.

Steiger writes in *The Other* that every person is a channel. "Each of us expresses individualized Divine Energy in one form or another. . . . Vibratory impulses can occur through sound, music, words, mental and physical images, and thoughts." He calls the folks who are contacted by entities and channel information from the stars, "psychonauts."

Channeling is not a new phenomenon, rather the latest version of an age-old practice. Throughout history certain gifted people have acted as intermediaries between the world of ordinary reality and the higher or spiritual realms. Records of spiritualists and mediums conveying information from Martian star-dwellers can be found from the mid-nineteenth century. Hilary Evans, a British UFO researcher, has unearthed the stories of several mediums, including those of Catherine Elise Muller, who lived in Geneva at the turn of the century and was able to speak in "Martian" (very similar to French); she described "how the Martians travel, what their homes are like, and so on." Just as the books of Jules Verne and H. G. Wells reflected the "images" of the "collective mind" during their time, Evans's mediums "lived at a

> *"You know, there are fewer than six people in this room who know the real story."*
>
> —Ronald Reagan to Steven Spielberg on the movie *E.T.* as it was being screened at the White House, and later recounted by Jaime Shandera

time when the idea of space travel, and particularly contact with Mars, was in the air."

In the modern UFO era, George Adamski, from Mount Palomar, California, was one of the first channels to gain notoriety and a major following. His alien contact, a Venusian named Orthon, taught him the "Science of Life" and secrets from the Studies of Cosmic Law. Adamski taught Cosmic Philosophy, dealing with space people and their plans that include "ending all warfare on Earth." His fame spread around the world, garnering him interviews with royalty and influential people. He published many books, including the best-selling cult classic *Flying Saucers Have Landed*.

George Van Tassel founded his center at Giant Rock in the Mojave Desert after claiming to be contacted by a group of Etherians called Ashtar, Zoltan, and Desca from the planet Shanchea. On advice from these space beings, he designed the Integraton, a device for retarding the aging process (never completed), and founded the College of Universal Wisdom and the annual Interplanetary Spacecraft Convention, which was active from 1954 to 1977.

In 1954 Ruth Norman had a vision of cosmic harmony and began channeling an entity known as the Archangel Uriel, who convinced her to open a center in El Cajon, California. Her contacts with the Space

> "We live at an extraordinary moment for the Earth at least—the first time that a species has become able to wipe itself out [and] the first time that a species has become able to journey to the planets and stars. . . . Every surviving civilization is obliged to become spacefaring—not because of exploratory or romantic zeal, but for the most practical reason imaginable, staying alive."
>
> —Carl Sagan, *Pale Blue Dot*, 1994

Brothers, representatives of the Intergalactic Federation, revealed to her that she must help raise the consciousness of the planet and prepare it for the arrival of the Intergalactic Confederation. They would come on thirty-two spaceships "to help this rapidly dying world . . . to teach mankind a better, a higher, and happier way of life."

Every summer, Dr. R. Leo Sprinkle sponsors the annual Rocky Mountain Conference on UFO Investigation, which attracts contactees from around the world to the University of Wyoming campus. Many of the attendees believe that the Galactic Federation—an extraterrestrial version of the United Nations—has placed them on this planet to spread the cosmic word and to prevent earthlings from destroying themselves with weapons and war.

In their book *The Unidentified*, authors Jerome Clark and Loren Coleman call these experiences of contact with aliens "Paraufology," or the "objective manifestations" of the UFO phenomenon. The voices and visions purported to come from alien visitors are, according to Clark and Coleman, "psychokinetically-generated by-products of those unconscious processes which shape a culture's vision of the Otherworld. Existing only temporarily, they are at best only quasi-physical."

> *"Now, I do believe there's intelligent life in the universe. With hundreds of millions of stars, all those galaxies that I talked about, some of those stars have to have planetary systems, some of those planets have to be in a position—like our Earth—to foster intelligent life. Not rudimentary life, but intelligent life. The question is, how can we get there, and are those civilizations a million years ahead of us, or a million years behind."*
>
> —Jim Lowell, astronaut and author of *Lost Moon*, 1994

The Parallel Search

The first visionary to suggest that ETs might eventually contact us via radio signals was the renowned inventor and radio pioneer of the 1930s, Nikola Tesla of Colorado. But it wasn't until 1959, the same year that *The Twilight Zone* premiered on television, that astronomer Frank Drake proposed using a new radio telescope at a premier national research facility to pursue the age-old questions: Where did we come from? Are we unique? What does it mean to be a human being?

Founded at the National Radio Astronomy Observatory in Green Bank, West Virginia, Project Ozma was named "after a land far away, difficult to reach, and populated by strange and exotic beings." Drake's goal was to search for extraterrestrial intelligence because, as he said, "I find nothing more tantalizing than the thought that radio messages from alien civilizations in space are passing through our offices and homes, right now, like a whisper we can't quite hear." His ardent belief as a scientist and a humanist was that "interstellar contact will enrich our

Photo courtesy of José Acevedo

Aerial photograph of the radio telescopes at Arecibo, Puerto Rico, where a team of scientists has transmitted a message to possible alien listeners in the constellation Hercules, 25,000 light-years away.

lives immeasurably" and that we will "witness the history of the future, not just the past."

According to the now famous "Drake Equation" of the 1960s, there are approximately 10,000 advanced extraterrestrial civilizations in the Milky Way Galaxy alone. To make contact with even one, he and his colleagues believe, would be the biggest event in history.

After reviewing recent advances in science, such as experiments tracing conceivable chemical pathways in which life might develop, observations of interstellar clouds, comets, and meteorites that confirm the basic chemical makeup of life throughout the universe, and the exploration of the "bewildering variety of planets and satellites just in our own system," Drake concluded in 1990 that his original estimation hasn't changed significantly.

In his avid search for "first contact," Drake believes he is staking out the middle ground between the mistaken notion that aliens have been visiting us for millennia, and the equally disturbing idea that they will seize control in the future. To do so, he reminds people that "even back-and-forth conversation with them is highly unlikely, since radio signals, traveling at the speed of light, take *years* to reach the nearest stars, and many *millennia* to get to the farthest ones, where advanced civilizations may reside. But one-way communication is a different story. . . ."

> *"First contact between two advanced technologies might well result in a fusion of knowledge that might benefit each one extremely."*
>
> —Isaac Asimov, scientist and author

Even though the first pictures that came back from outer space and the moon were fuzzy, blurry, and gray, they conveyed the danger, awe, and wonder necessary to fuel the fires of imagination. By early 1995, the high-tech color photographs being beamed back from space shuttle flights are showing images of a pure celestial ballet that is stirring the world's soul once more.

As the millennium approaches, we continue to search the heavens for other life-forms and answers to the ancient questions about the origins of life. And as we do, we're finding that the very act of exploration can be a dance that revitalizes our lives here on earth.

"[Of] the UFOs . . . one thing is certain: they have become a living myth. *We have a golden opportunity of seeing how a legend is formed, and how in a difficult and dark time for humanity a miraculous tale grows up of an attempted intervention by extraterrestrial 'heavenly' powers— and this at the very time when human fantasy is seriously considering the possibility of space travel and of visiting or even invading other planets."*

—Carl Gustav Jung, *Flying Saucers*

A Presidential View

"One fall evening in 1969, Georgia governor Jimmy Carter was outdoors preparing for a speech in the little town of Leary when he—and about a dozen other witnesses—spotted a bright object in the western sky. Carter described it as self-luminous, about the size of the moon, and sometimes stationary, sometimes moving forward and backward. He took it to be a UFO and reported the sighting to the National Investigations Committee on Aerial Phenomena. Several years later, when Carter was president of the United States, his science advisor suggested to NASA that a new investigation of UFOs be launched. The space agency declined."

—The UFO Phenomenon

"I'll make every piece of information this country has about UFOs available to the public and the scientists."

—President Jimmy Carter,
London Daily Telegraph, June 2, 1979

Organizations with Information on the Scientific Search for Extraterrestrial Intelligence

The Astronomical Society of the Pacific
390 Ashton Avenue
San Francisco, CA 94112

The Planetary Society
65 North Catalina Avenue
Pasadena, CA 91106

The SETI Institute
2035 Landings Drive
Mountain View, CA 94043

Book Guide

First Contact:
The Search for Extraterrestrial Intelligence
edited by Ben Bova and Byron Preiss
(NAL Books, 1990)

In Advance of the Landing:
Folk Concepts of Outer Space
Douglas Curran (Abbeville Press, 1985)

The Twilight Zone Companion
Marc Scott Zicree (Silman-James Press, 1982)

Understanding the Present:
Science and the Soul of Man
Bryan Appleyard (Anchor Books, 1993)

Epilogue

Every age has the Stonehenge it desires and deserves.
      —Jacquetta Hawkes, *God in the Machine*

After nearly fifty years no one can claim to know exactly what these strange entities called UFOs are, or why they are appearing in our skies, or even why people respond to them the way they do. "When the solution to the UFO puzzle comes, I think it will prove not to be just a step in the march of science but a quantum jump," J. Allen Hynek wrote in the October 1985 issue of the *International UFO Journal*.

Until then, perhaps the best we can do is consider a "wave of possibilities," as the physicists do when trying to determine why subatomic particles play footloose and fancy-free with the laws of space and time. Symbolic or real? Angels or aliens? Archetypes or spaceships? Hallucinations or visionary encounters? Science-fiction fantasy or hints of time travel? Psychic disturbances or clues to our evolutionary future? The cosmic paradox revealed by modern science and depth psychology suggests *both* and more. Cultural historian Keith Thompson speculates that the UFO may be "two sides of a larger coin of a larger realm," and asks, "Are we as much a part of their dreams and myths as they are of ours?"

Ever elusive, ever changing, ever tantalizing, the UFO phenomenon is a "cosmic chameleon," in Thompson's memorable phrase, one that reminds us of our transcendent possibilities and urges us to expand our notions of reality. It is a collective dream fired by personal passions.

Still, the question remains: After the already mind-boggling mix of tragedy and triumph that has been revealed in the twentieth century, from the agonies of Hiroshima and the ecstasies of the fall of the Berlin Wall, from the barrage of bafflements in cosmology to the mind-bending ideas of quantum physics, would things change any more dramatically if we had irrefutable proof of space-and-time-defying alien-piloted flying saucers? Would it be the sky-shattering event that could threaten society and religion as we know it? Are we on the verge of calamity or on the edge of a great breakthrough in human consciousness?

Regardless of the origins of the bewildering lights and strange visitations, the very act of once again seriously contemplating the luminous displays in the night sky and the reports of shadowy presences that many people encounter on remote country roads or in their bedrooms has accomplished the trick of reenchanting the world for millions who believed that modern life was becoming soulless and devoid of mystery.

As we approach the millennium, we can look back over five decades that encompass the UFO phenomenon and know that the way we view the universe has dramatically changed. Mac Brazel, the man who stumbled across the mysterious debris outside of Roswell, New Mexico, summed it up when he confessed to a reporter, "Our lives will never be the same again."

How we view the magnitude of change in these unprecedented times and how we tell our story is how we live our lives. In the immortal words of Oscar Wilde, "We are all of us in the gutter, but some of us are looking at the stars."

And there, gazing in stillness and silence at the signs from the heavens, once again we can be perpetually astonished by life.

Guide to UFO Organizations and Media Resources

UFO Research Organizations, Membership Groups, and Clubs

CAUS
(Citizens Against UFO Secrecy)
P.O. Box 218
Coventry, CT 06238
Since 1978
Publication: *Just Cause* (quarterly).
This nonprofit organization is dedicated to recovering documents relating to government involvement in UFO investigations and research.

CSETI
(The Center for the Study of Extraterrestrial Intelligence)
P.O. Box 15401
Asheville, NC 28813
704/254–9650
Since 1990
Publication: a quarterly newsletter.
A nonprofit international scientific research organization dedicated to investigating extraterrestrial intelligence.

CSICOP (Committee for the Scientific Investigation of Claims of the Paranormal)
P.O. Box 703
Buffalo, NY 14226-0703
716/636–1425
Since 1976
This nonprofit organization investigates paranormal claims and UFO-related activity.

CUFOS
(J. Allen Hynek Center for UFO Studies)
2457 West Peterson Avenue
Chicago, IL 60659
312/271–3611
Since 1973
Publications: *International UFO Reporter* (bimonthly),
The Journal of UFO Studies (annual).
CUFOS is an international group of scientists, academics, investigators, and volunteers dedicated to the continuing examination and analysis of the UFO phenomenon. They serve as a clearinghouse for the two-way exchange of information, where UFO experiences can be reported and researched. They also maintain one of the world's largest collections of original data about the UFO phenomenon, including sightings and contacts, along with a large library of related books and magazines. CUFOS has a national network of field investigators to interview witnesses and examine physical evidence. They promote public understanding of the UFO phenomenon through their publications and public engagements.

INFO
(International Fortean Organization)
P.O. Box 367
Arlington, VA 22210-0367
703/522–9232
Since 1965
Publication: *INFO Journal* (quarterly).
The nonprofit organization was founded for the education and scientific study of "Fortean" phenomena, paranormal and anomalous phenomena that defy natural explanation. They investigate all strange and unexplainable events—including UFO sightings. (Each fall, they hold an annual convention, Fort Fest, in the Washington D.C. area.)

MUFON
(Mutual UFO Network, Inc.)
103 Oldtowne Road
Seguin, TX 78155-4099
512/379–9216
Since 1969
Publications: *MUFON Field Investigator's Manual;*
MUFON International UFO Symposium Proceedings
(annual); *MUFON UFO Journal* (monthly).
MUFON, the "world's largest UFO membership organization," is an international scientific network of
people seriously interested in studying and research-
ing the UFO phenomenon. They sponsor and
conduct worldwide conferences, seminars, and sym-
posiums, including the annual International UFO
Symposium. MUFON trains UFO field investigators, directs amateur radio networks to receive and
disseminate UFO sighting reports, and publishes a
comprehensive guide available to anyone interested
in conducting UFO investigations. MUFONET is
their computer BBS (bulletin board system) on the
Internet.

NICUFO
(National Investigations Committee on UFOs)
P.O. Box 73
Van Nuys, CA 91408-0073
818/989–5942
Since 1967
Publications: *Inter-Space-Link Confidential Newsletter*
(monthly); *UFO Journal* (quarterly).
A nonprofit organization dedicated to UFO, space,
and science research and education. NICUFO hosts
seminars and maintains a large collection of UFO
photos, books, and other materials.

SSE
(Society for Scientific Exploration)
P.O. Box 3818
University Station
Charlottesville, VA 22903-0818
804/924–4905
Since 1982
Publication: *Journal of Scientific Exploration*
(quarterly).
With its members mostly from scientific and academic communities, the group investigates anomalous phenomena, including UFOs, to gain further understanding and share their knowledge with the public.

UFO Conferences

Gulf Breeze UFO Conference
(held in October)
Contact: Project Awareness
P.O. Box 730
Gulf Breeze, FL 32562
904/432–8888

International MUFON Symposium
(held in July)
Contact: MUFON
103 Oldtowne Road
Seguin, TX 78155-4099
512/379–9216

International UFO Congress
(held in November)
4266 Broadway
Oakland, CA 94611
510/428–0340

National UFO Conference
(held in September)
Contact: UAPA (United Aerial Phenomenon
Agency) and *Flying Saucer Digest*
P.O. Box 347032
Cleveland, OH 44134-7032
216/631–6356

NICUFO Annual Conference
Contact: NICUFO (National Investigations
Committee on UFOs)
P.O. Box 73
Van Nuys, CA 91408-0073
818/989–5942

Rocky Mountain UFO Conference
(held in June)
IFUFOCS (Institute for UFO Contactee
Studies)
1425 Steele Street
Laramie, WY 82070
307/745–7897, 307/721–5125

San Francisco Expo West
(held in November)
P.O. Box 1011
Pacific Palisades, CA 90272
415/905–8874

UFO/Alien/E.T. & Abduction Congress
(held in March)
UFO hot line: 609/888–1358

The UFO Experience Annual Conference
Contact: Omega Communications
P.O. Box 2051
Cheshire, CT 06410

Whole Life Expos are held annually around the country. They present UFO guest speakers and offer presentations on UFOs.
For information, call 800/332–0099.

Magazines

Continuum (quarterly)
MICAP (Multi-national Investigations
Cooperative on Aerial Phenomena)/ParaNet
P.O. Box 172
Wheat Ridge, CO 80034-0172
303/431–8796
Always "Answering Questions, Questioning Answers," ParaNet is a global computer network specializing in the paranormal.

Fate (monthly)
84 South Wabasha Street
St. Paul, MN 55107
612/291–1070
Disseminates information on unusual topics, including UFOs.

Flying Saucer Digest (quarterly)
UAPA (United Aerial Phenomenon Agency)
P.O. Box 347032
Cleveland, OH 44134-7032
216/631–6356

The International UFO Library Magazine
(quarterly)
11684 Ventura Boulevard, Suite 708
Studio City, CA 91604
818/769–2917
Reports news and information on UFOs and ETs.

Skeptical Inquirer
CSICOP (Committee for the Scientific Investigation of Claims of the Paranormal)
P.O. Box 703
Buffalo, NY 14226-0703
716/636–1425; fax 716/636–1733
"Separates fact from fiction from today's flood of occult and pseudo-scientific thinking."

Skeptics UFO Newsletter
404 N Street SW
Washington D.C. 20024
From the skeptical point of view, an analysis of issues and opinions in current ufology.

Strange (biannual)
P.O. Box 2246
Rockville, MD 20847
301/460–4789; fax 301/460–1959
Covers strange phenomena from around the world, including UFOs.

UFO (bimonthly)
P.O. Box 1053
Sunland, CA 91041-1053
818/951–1250
Handles "UFOs Tonite" radio talk show.

UFO: A Forum on Extraordinary Theories and Phenomena (bimonthly)
818/951–1250

UFO Encounters (monthly)
Aztec Publishing
P.O. Box 1142
Norcross, GA 30091
404/279–1732

The UFO Enigma (monthly)
P.O. Box 31544
St. Louis, MO 63131
314/946–4095

The UFOlogist (monthly)
North Bridge Corporation
P.O. Box 1359
Palatka, FL 32178
904/325–9851

UFO Report (monthly)
The Romadka Printing System
P.O. Box 1144
Marshfield, WI 54449

UFO Alien Encounters (bimonthly)
UFOs Unexplained Universe (bimonthly)
UFO Universe (bimonthly)
Unsolved UFO Sightings (bimonthly)
GC Publishing Group, Inc.
1700 Broadway
New York, NY 10019

UFO Resources

Arcturus Books, Inc.
1443 SE Port St. Lucie Boulevard
Port St. Lucie, FL 34952
407/398–0796
Publication: Catalog.
Has a wide selection of UFO-related books, magazines, and tapes.

Inner Light Publications
P.O. Box 753
New Brunswick, NJ 08903
Publications: *Inner Light* (monthly); *UFO Review.*
Books and materials related to UFOs. Sponsors
UFO conferences.

Lightworks Audio & Video
P.O. Box 661593
Los Angeles, CA 90066
310/398–4949
Publication: Catalog.
Offers a wide selection of UFO-related books, maga-
zines, and audio- and videotapes.

UFO Audio-Video Clearing House
P.O. Box 342-AL
Yucaipa, CA 92399-0342
714/795–3611
Has archived UFO-related radio and television pro-
grams dating back to the 1950s.

UFOIRC
(UFO Information Retrieval Center)
313 West Cochise Drive #158
Phoenix, AZ 85051-9501
612/997–1523
Collects, analyzes, publishes, and disseminates information about UFOs.

UFO News Clipping Services

UFONS (UFO Newsclipping Service)
Route 1
Box 220
Plumerville, AK 85754-5014
Monthly report of worldwide UFO news clippings.

Worldwide UFO Newsclipping Bureau and
Public Information Center
955 West Lancaster Road, Suite 420
Orlando, FL 32809
Monthly report of worldwide UFO news clippings;
audio and video.

UFO Media

"UFOs Tonite"
This weekly radio talk show is hosted by *UFO* magazine's research director, Don Ecker, and airs on Saturday from 9 P.M. to 11 P.M. (Pacific Standard Time). For information on how to find it in your area, call 818/951–1250. The show's call-in number is 800/336–2225.

International UFO Organizations

Australia

ACUFOS (Australian Centre for UFO Studies)
P.O. Box 728
Lane Cove, New South Wales
Australia 2066

UFORA (UFO Research Australia)
P.O. Box 2435
Cairns, Queensland
Australia 4870

VUFORS (Victorian UFO Research Society)
P.O. Box 43
Moorabbin, Victoria
Australia 3189

Canada

Alberta UFO Study Group
P.O. Box 38044, Capilano Postal Outlet
Edmonton, Alberta
Canada T6A 0Y0

CUFORN (Canadian UFO Research Network)
Box 15, Station A
Willowdale, Ontario
Canada M2N 5S7

UFORIC (UFO Research Institute of Canada)
Dept 25
1665 Robson Street
Vancouver, British Columbia
Canada V6G 3C2

UFOROM (UFOlogy Research of Manitoba)
P.O. Box 1918
Winnipeg, Manitoba
Canada R3C 3R2

Great Britain

ASSAP (The Association for the Scientific Study of Anomalous Phenomena)
20 Paul Street
Frome, Somerset
England BA11 1DX

BUFORA (British UFO Research Association)
2C Leyton Road, Suite 1
Harpenden, Herts
England AL5 2TL

Contact International
11 Ouseley Close
New Marston, Oxford
England 0X3 0JS

NUFON (Northern UFO Network)
37 Heathbank Road
Stockport, Cheshire
England SK3 0UP
Serves as an alliance for UFO groups in northern England and Scotland.

Quest International
18, Hardy Meadows
Grassington, Near Skipton
North Yorkshire
England BD23 5LR

SRUFO (Scottish UFO Research)
129 Langton View
East Calder, West Lothian
Scotland EH53 ORE

For a comprehensive listing of regional and international UFO organizations, contact the publishers of the *Almanac of UFO Organizations & Publications:*
Phaedra Enterprises
P.O. Box 1241
San Bruno, CA 94066

Online Services

Are you an Internet cruiser? Here's a sampling of electronic resources, online ufozines, newsgroups, and bulletin board services (BBS):

CUFON (Computer UFO Network) BBS
206/776–0382

MUFON MUFONET BBS
512/379–9216

International Fortean Organization
FORTNET BBS
703/522–9232

Fortean Research Center BBS
206/488–2587

ParaNet BBS
303/431–8797

Newsgroups with UFO topics:
alt.alien.visitor
alt.paranet.abduct
alt.paranet.ufo
alt.paranormal
talk.religion.newage

"High strangeness" articles and UFO FAQs (frequently asked questions) are available at these sites:
Telnet Address: bbs.isca.uiowa.edu

FTP Address: ftp.spies.com
Path: /Library/Fringe/UFO

FTP Address: grind.isca.uowa.edu
Path: /info/paranet

Gopher Address: wiretap.spies.com
Wiretap Online Library
Path: Fringes or
Path: ufos

FTP Address: ftp.uu.net
Path: /doc/literary/obi/ufo

FTP Address: info.rutgers.edu
Path: /pub/ufo

Members of the Intergalactic Federation, walk-ins, and hybrids are welcome to learn more about our Space Brothers from Venus and Orion at this World Wide Web URL:
http://err.ethz.ch/~kiwi/Spirit/starbuilders.html

Ever thought about interstellar travel? Everything you always wanted to know.
World Wide Web URL:
http://err.ethz.ch/~kiwi/Spirit/RKMCorner/spaceships.html

Obscure Research Labs (ORL) Online:
ORL@cup.portal.com

Society for Scientific Exploration (SSE):
LWF@Virginia.edu

Alberta UFO Study Group:
e-mail address: CompuServe 71543,3524 (Canada)

Ufology Research of Manitoba (UFOROM) will
send you an electronic issue of their *Swamp Gas
Journal* if you e-mail a request to:
rutkows@ccu.umanitoba.ca

Groom Lake Desert Rat
Internet e-mail address: psychospy@aol.com
Online magazine published by our friends keeping
tabs on the military's secret goings-on at Area 51.
Are they testing captured spacecraft, or building the
stealth bomber of tomorrow?

ISCNI
**(Institute for the Study of Contact with Non-
human Intelligence)**
3463 State Street #440
Santa Barbara, CA 93105
800/41–ISCNI; fax 805/563–8503
ISCNI's vision is to provide the most credible and
impactful information available concerning human
contact with nonhuman intelligence. Cofounded by
UFO researcher Michael Lindemann.
America Online e-mail address: ISCNI
Internet e-mail address: iscni@aol.com
Keyword: EUN

The X-Files Newsgroup: alt.tv.x-files
Where X-philes (fans) meet to talk about their favorite show.
World Wide Web URL: http://alfred1.u.washington.edu:8080/~roland/x-files/x-files.html
If you subscribe to Delphi Internet you'll find the special X-Files Forum. You can download *X-Files* photos and videos, chat with the creators, and more. 800/695–4005.

Star Trek FTP Address: ftp.uu.net
A Trekkie's delight.
Path: /doc/literary/obi/Star.Trek.Stories
Path: /usenet/rec.arts.startrek/
Telnet Address: panda.uiowa.edu

Newsgroup: alt.fan.
Where you can talk about your favorite TV characters.

Newsgroup: rec.arts.sf.tv
Science-fiction TV shows

World Wide Web URL:
http://akebono.stanford.edu/yahoo/Entertainment/Television/Science_Fiction/

Newsgroup: rec.arts.sf.movies
Science-fiction movies

UFO Research Funding

FUFOR
(The Fund for UFO Research, Inc.)
P.O. Box 277
Mt. Rainier, MD 20712
A nonprofit organization that provides grants for scientific research and public education projects dealing with the UFO phenomenon.

Guide to
Common
UFO Terms

Abductee. A person who believes they have been kidnapped by extraterrestrial aliens. Through the help of hypnosis, abductees often recover information about their experiences. Many have formed support groups. Abductees often prefer to be known as **experiencers.**

Abductee Implant. Some abductees show physical evidence of their experiences through scars, wounds, or implants they say they received as a result of physical examinations and operations performed by aliens.

Abduction. A controversial and growing phenomenon in ufology, involving UFO witnesses who claim to have been transported from their car or their bedroom and into alien spacecraft, usually at night.

Alien. The term "space alien" refers to a being believed to be of extraterrestrial origin, or at least alien to the human race. Some who claim to have encountered these beings use the word "alien" to describe hostile or dark entities and the term **"ET"** to refer to the more benevolent entities.

Amnesiac Block. The belief that alien entities have replaced an abductee's memory with a substitute memory that cloaks the event and which can only be removed through hypnotic regression therapy or by the ETs themselves. Also called **screen memory** or **substitute image.**

Ball Lightning. A rare atmospheric phenomenon similar to regular lightning except that it glows in a spherical shape and moves slowly. Attempts have been made to interpret many UFO reports as ball lightning.

Channel. A person who conveys thoughts or energy from a source believed to be outside the person's body or conscious mind. Some channelers believe they receive messages from extraterrestrials. Also called **trance channelers** and **mediums.**

Cone of Silence. Some abductees describe a period of profound silence occurring just before and during their abductions.

Contactee. One who claims to have been contacted by or shared a personal exchange with extraterrestrial beings.

Crawl-In. According to spiritualists who believe humans have a higher "intergalactic purpose," crawl-ins are those who have entered this dimension through the normal birth process.

Cult Group. Many groups of ET enthusiasts and contactee cults have been formed around the UFO phenomenon since the 1950s. A common thread among members is that their belief is based more on information from a cosmic visionary or channeler, than on hard scientific facts. The groups often have an ecological basis and promote "intergalactic peace."

Debunking. The outright rejection of all or part of the UFO phenomenon. Debunkers tend to lack the analysis or study to back their claims, leading serious ufologists to speculate about their motives. Government and scientific bodies are the usual debunkers, as well as individuals who have a personal agenda or desire to be in the limelight.

Disinformation/Misinformation. Refers to the practice of duping the public (or the enemy) by substituting accurate information with bunk information. Conspiracy theorists believe that various government agencies spread disinformation about UFOs in order to get ufologists off the right track and onto a false one.

Earthlight. Balls of light that are reported in areas experiencing earthquake activity.

EBE (Extraterrestrial Biological Entity). Beings with a carbon-based biological makeup similar to humans, who are believed to be of extraterrestrial origin.

EM (Electro-Magnetic Effect). A theory that some UFOs are produced by the physical force of electro-magnetism.

ETH (Extraterrestrial Hypothesis). Especially popular in the Americas, this theory claims that UFOs are of extraterrestrial origin and aliens are visitors from another world.

Fireball. A ball of fire, or something resembling a ball, glowing in the sky like a brilliant meteor. This is one theory of explanation for some UFOs.

Flap. When numerous UFO sightings have been reported in a particular area.

Flying Saucer. This popular term used to describe UFOs came into common usage after Kenneth Arnold's now-infamous sighting near Mount Rainier in 1947.

Foo Fighter. World War II fighter pilots coined this term to describe the balls or disks of light many reported to have seen following or interfering with their aircraft. At first thought to be an enemy force, it was later reported that German pilots had made similar claims, as did pilots flying in the Korean conflict.

Ghost Rocket. A "pre-saucer" term used in the 1930s and 1940s to describe the cigar-shaped lights or craft reported mostly in Norway and Sweden.

Hybrid. In the UFO context, a hybrid is believed to be the offspring of two beings from different planets of origin. A being that is half-human, half-ET.

Hypnotic Regression. A psychotherapy treatment that facilitates analysis by means of hypnosis, and is believed by some to recover memories of traumatic events.

IFO (Identified Flying Object). Between 90 and 95 percent of all UFO sighting reports are eventually identifiable—whether they be explained by naturally occurring phenomena, aircraft lights, distant stars, searchlights, etc.

Interdimensional/Ultradimensional. Alien entities believed to be from parallel universes or another dimension of reality or time altogether.

Intergalactic Federation. A group that some contactees and fans of channeled entities believe is made up of representatives from many planets.

Lenticular Cloud. A naturally occurring yet rare phenomenon, this type of cloud has a lens (or lentil) shape and sometimes generates UFO reports.

Ley Line. Part of a theory used to explain the alignment or "grid of power" of ancient sacred sites, stone circles, and megaliths. Also called dragon paths.

LGM (Little Green Men). A snide term skeptics often use when referring to extraterrestrials, it's imbued with preconceptions of fairy tales and leprechauns. In truth, alien beings are rarely described as green.

Meteor. Phenomenon that occurs in the atmosphere, noticeable to the naked eye as streaks of glowing light in the sky. If one reaches the earth without being completely vaporized, it is a **meteorite.** Both have been used to explain certain UFO sightings.

MIB (Men in Black). Stories of well-dressed, sometimes short, men in dark suits appearing directly after UFO sightings were frequently reported in the early years of the UFO phenomenon. Theories as to who these men were range from intimidating FBI agents to aliens themselves.

Millennium. A period of 1,000 years. We are now approaching the end of a millennium, and the next one begins in 2001. Various religious and spiritual groups attach a great significance to this marking of time.

Mock Suns. Phenomenon that occurs when there appear to be two or more suns in the sky. The imitation suns can be formed by the reflections of light off of ice or water. Also called **sun dogs** or **parhelia.**

MTE (Missing Time Experience). The phenomenon used to explain why UFO witnesses report losing time.

NDE (Near-Death Experience). The state of consciousness and sequence of common experiences had by many hospital patients who had been declared clinically dead, but then returned to life. They include having an **OOBE (Out-of-Body Experience),** seeing visions of spiritual beings, and embracing a warm, bright tunnel of light.

Paranormal. The kind of phenomena that are outside the range of normal experience afforded by the five senses, stretching the abilities of empirical science to measure.

Phantasmagoria. Constantly shifting complex successions or displays of optical effects and illusions, seen or imagined.

Phenomenon (plural: **phenomena**). Rare or significant observable fact or event; an object or aspect known through the senses rather than by thought or intuition; a temporal or spatiotemporal object of sensory experience.

Sighting. The event of seeing a UFO.

Skywatcher. A UFO enthusiast who watches the skies for UFOs and other atmospheric phenomena. Some skywatchers make long pilgrimages to UFO hot spots in the hope of witnessing secrets from the sky.

Space Brother. A friendly visitor from another planet.

UAO (Unexplained Aerial Object). Another term for a UFO, or unidentified flying object.

UAP (Unidentified Atmospheric Phenomenon). A term that is applied to a UFO that has been determined to be a naturally occurring phenomenon rather than a spaceship.

UFO (Unidentified Flying Object). Any aerial or celestial object or light discovered visually or by radar, but not immediately understood or identified. According to Hynek, first used in 1952.

Ufocal/Window Area. A place where rashes of UFO sightings have been reported.

Ufology. The study of the UFO phenomenon, a discipline that can encompass many scientific fields—from astrophysics to engineering, biology to psychosociology, meteorology to cosmology.

Uforia. The state of elation about the phantasmagoric mysteries of unidentified flying objects, abductions, aliens, and other celestial and extraterrestrial phenomena.

UUO (Underwater Unidentified Objects). As the field of oceanography grows, so do the number of unidentifiable objects seen underwater.

Vehicle Interference. The stalling or complete stoppage of a vehicle's engine, often included in reports of UFO close encounters.

Walk-In. Some ETH proponents believe that alien entities can take over a human persona, in effect entering into a human body and assuming a human identity. Some ET channelers insist that an alien entity cannot enter a person's body unless it is fully agreed upon by the person. Some ET channelers believe they are walk-ins and are more enlightened than the average earthling due to their "interdimensional consciousness."

Phil Cousineau is an award-winning author and filmmaker whose lifelong fascination with phenomenal realities has taken him on journeys around the world. He is a cultural historian and popular lecturer on a wide range of topics, from mythology and movies to creativity and soul. His books include: *Prayers at 3 a.m.*; *Soul: An Archaeology: Readings from Socrates to Ray Charles*; *The Soul of the World* (with Eric Lawton); *Deadlines: A Rhapsody on a Theme of Famous and Infamous Last Words*; and *The Hero's Journey: Joseph Campbell on His Life and Work*.

Cousineau currently lives in San Francisco.

Author during 1994 visit to the UFO Enigma Museum in Roswell, New Mexico.

Author's Note

While every effort has been made to assure the accuracy of the information herein, the nature of the world is mutable and mercurial, and addresses change. If you would like to send in any comments about what is printed here or update information for future printings, please send a card to:

UFOs
298 Fourth Avenue, Box 417
San Francisco, CA 94118